# MAHDI:
## THE GUIDED ONE

*HISTORY & CONTROVERSY*

ALEXANDER EKWALL

ISBN-13: 978-0-578-48262-0

# DEDICATION

This book is dedicated first and foremost to my wife Megan Ekwall, but also to anyone willing and capable of communicating religion without the intention of defining who is right and who is wrong.

# CONTENTS

| | | |
|---|---|---|
| | Preface | 6 |
| | Introduction | 8 |
| 1 | The Objective of Al-Mahdi | 10 |
| 2 | Family History | 14 |
| 3 | If He Is Alive, Where Is He? | 21 |
| 4 | Historical Mahdis | 25 |
| | 4. 1 Muhammad Jaunpuri | 26 |
| | 4.2 Siyyid `Alí Muḥammad Shírází | 29 |
| | 4.3 Muhammad Ahmad | 54 |
| | 4.4 Mirza Ghulam Ahmad | 70 |
| | Conclusion | 82 |
| | Index | 90 |

# PREFACE

I would like to preface this by saying that although I am not a Muslim, nor an adherent of any religion, I undertook the task of writing this book in the hopes of being able to present the material in a way that both Muslims and non-Muslims would find fair. The aim of this text is not to persuade one to become an adherent of the Islamic Faith, nor is it intended to sway one away from the Islamic Faith, but rather to merely present the material in a way that accurately represents the history of Imam Mahdi in the Islamic world. My interest in the subject arose out of curiosity, as with most things, and given I already had an interest in the history of religion and mythology undertaking the writing of this book just came naturally.

Aside from the newsletter that I started back in February of 2016 called *Omnia: A Little Bit of Everything*, this is my first published work, and it would not have come to fruition without the help of my editor Megan Ekwall. Megan, my incredible wife, has helped place me in the position I am in today that allowed me to write this book. I'd like to thank my mother for always being there and of course for having supported my interest in literature from before I could even read the contents of a Dr. Seuss book. I thank my good friend Slade for his assistance with the cover of this book and for always having a solution to any difficulties I had along the way. My gratitude toward the publisher CreateSpace/KDP cannot go without mention either. I may not know the names of those individuals who helped make this happen at CreateSpace/KDP, given our need for communication was minimal, but I am grateful for all they have done to make this book available to all who wish to read it.

# INTRODUCTION

Muhammad al-Mahdi, often just referred to as Imam Mahdi, is a figure within Islam whose identity is the subject of much debate. It is believed that only Allah truly knows who he is. Before delving into the many opinions surrounding Muhammad al-Mahdi, there are a few terms that should be discussed: Sunni, Shia, and Imam/Imamate.

Within the Muslim community there are two primary sects; the Sunni and the Shia, with the main difference between the two being their views on the Imamate. The Imamate consists of those who became leaders over the Muslim community following the death of the Holy Prophet Muhammad. The common belief among Sunni Muslims is that the twelfth Imam has not yet appeared and that his identity is known only by Allah, whereas the conventional view among Shia Muslims is that the twelfth Imam has been born and remains alive to this day. Under the assumption that Muhammad al-Mahdi is still among us, the question becomes; where is he? There are many opinions on this matter, but none have transcended the status of opinion and become fact. When seeking the whereabouts of someone who may not even still be alive, we must ask ourselves when to stop looking, because if he has expired, we are asking ourselves a question without an answer. Regardless of whether Muhammad al-Mahdi has already lived, is currently alive, or has yet to come, a belief present among both major Muslim sects is that *the* Mahdi will emerge/reemerge at the end of time.

# I
# THE OBJECTIVE OF AL-MAHDI

Before getting immersed in this whirlwind of who the Mahdi might be and from what period he belongs, it is essential to begin by understanding what his purpose is. The easiest way to go about this is to start with the name al-Mahdi itself, which translates to 'The Directed One,' otherwise known as a Messiah.[1] In identifying the translation, it is easier to understand that although in many cases mention of Imam Mahdi is referring to a specific individual, the honorific itself is more general.

A passage from the writings of Ayatollah Baqir al-Sadr (d. A. D. 1980) and Ayatollah Murtadha Mutahhari (d. A. D. 1979) describes the significance of al-Mahdi by stating "A figure more legendary than that of the Mahdi, the Awaited Saviour, has not been seen in the history of mankind."[2] Although there have been multiple messianic claims throughout history, a few of which are discussed in Chapter IV, the

---

[1] *"An Encyclopedia of Religions"* p. 228-29.

[2] "The Awaited Saviour" Prologue.

significance of the Mahdi is one that cannot be rejected by the Muslim community. A figure known as Jesus Christ may be among the closest comparisons in the Western hemisphere, and when looking at the objective of Imam Mahdi, it is easy to see some similarities. For instance, a common belief among Muslims is that al-Mahdi will appear/reappear at the end of time to establish justice throughout the world, while Christians believe in the reappearance of Christ on Judgement Day to punish sinners and reward those who did right, effectively establishing justice as well. The difference is that al-Mahdi will be accompanied by the prophet Isa. Isa, often translated as *Jesus Christ*, differs from the Christian image of Christ in one big way; Isa was never crucified. Otherwise many similarities remain, such as both having a virgin mother named Mary/Maryam. This is by no means the only instance of similarities between Islam and Christianity considering that both are Abrahamic religions that acknowledge some of the same prophets; such as Abraham, Moses, and Noah. One significant difference is that in Islam, Jesus Christ is considered a past prophet, which is not the case in Christianity.

At the time of al-Mahdi's appearance/reappearance at the end of time, it is believed that Jesus Christ will descend from heaven to follow al-Mahdi in prayer for the Muslims and will also assist in defeating Al-Masih ad-Dajjal[3], otherwise known as the Antichrist. Although this is the more widely accepted view, as shared by the Egyptian scholar Al-Suyuti (d. A. D. 1505) who has been known to defend the tradition of Jesus following al-Mahdi in prayer, it has not been met without

---

[3] A description of Dajjal can be seen in a hadith collection compiled by Muhammad al-Bukhari (d. A. D. 870) in volume 4 verse 649 of *Ṣaḥīḥ al-Bukhārī* (*Hadith of Bukhari*) where the Prophet Muhammad describes Dajjal as "blind in the right eye and his eyes look like a bulging out grape." If one were to continue reading this hadith one would find the description of a dream that Prophet Muhammad had where Dajjal was seen playing the role of the false messiah.

opposition. Polymath Sa'ad al-Din Taftazani (d. A. D. 1390), although among the few, has been known to voice disagreement with this belief, as he suggests that the accounts of this tradition are unreliable.[4]

Ka'ab al-Ahbar[5] (d. A. D. 653), an early Jewish convert to Islam, claims that the Mahdi is the man on the white horse seen in the Book of Revelation in the Holy Bible. This is referring to chapter 6 verse 2 where it states:

"And I saw, and behold a white horse: and he that sat on him had a bow; and a crown was given unto him: and he went forth conquering, and to conquer."

To many, this claim may seem absurd, but there may be a reasonable explanation for why it came to be. When al-Mahdi is to appear/reappear, he is to lead armies, hence the bow and mention of conquering. The crown also alludes to the belief that al-Mahdi shall rule for seven to nine years upon his arrival. Although in Christianity this verse would suggest a victory for the followers of Christ, in the case of the claim made by Ka'ab al-Ahbar it would merely indicate a victory for al-Mahdi and Isa.

"Among his [Mahdi's] tasks was the revival of Islam, the conversion of the world, and the unification of all religions."[6]

The final perspective, one that I personally do not endorse based strictly on the fact that its acceptance will likely only lead to further hostility toward the Islamic Faith, is that al-Mahdi and Isa play the role of Antichrist and false prophet respectively, mentioned in the Holy Bible. The objective of

---

[4] "*The Promised Savior*" p. 38.

[5] "*Antichrist: Islam's Awaited Messiah*" Ch. 4 p.28.

[6] "*Mirza Ghulam Ahmad of Qadian*" p. xi.

al-Mahdi, in this case, would be to lure in the followers of the *true* Jesus Christ so that when he appears he will be the one regarded as the false prophet, thus allowing the Jews and Christians to fall into the hands of Satan through the works of al-Mahdi and Isa.

I will not attempt to discredit the claims of one religion by referencing claims/allegations made by another religion. For this reason, this perspective will not be covered in detail. For the sake of showing an array of views on the purpose of al-Mahdi, it only seemed right that this argument should at least be noted, as there are likely many who are of this opinion. Overall, throughout Islamic scripture, the purpose of al-Mahdi is to bring justice, rule for seven to nine years, and with the help of Isa, defeat Dajjal.

# II
# FAMILY HISTORY

After discussing the purpose of al-Mahdi in a broader sense, what better way to continue than by taking a closer look at who Imam Mahdi is as an individual as seen from the Shia perspective. The writings of Abu Dawood[7] (d. A. D. 889) serve as the starting point for understanding al-Mahdi's lineage. He records that Umm Salama/Hind bint Abi Umayya (d. A. D. 680) heard her husband, the Holy Prophet Muhammad (d. A. D. 632), refer to Mahdi as a descendant of Fatimah. Fatimah is the Holy Prophet Muhammad's daughter. Before undertaking the task of following Imam Mahdi's family history, it is important to clarify the difference between the Shia and Sunni views of the Imamate.

The Shi'as, often referred to as Shi'ites, only account for roughly 10% of the Muslim community, whereas Sunnis, often referred to as Sunnites, account for about 90%. The term Shi'a originates from the root *Sha'a*, meaning to follow,

---

[7] *"English Translation of Sunan Abu Dawud"* Vol. 4, p. 508.

conform with, or to obey[8] while the term Sunni originates from *Al-as-Sunna* meaning 'people of the Sunna(h).'[9] John Norman Hollister, author of *The Shi'a of India*, introduces the Shia's by quoting the Spanish Islamic scholar Ibn Hazm (d. A.D. 1064):

"He who agrees with the Shi'ite that 'Ali is the most excellent of men after the Prophet, and that he and his descendants after him are worthier of the Imamate than [anyone], is a Shi'ite[...]"[10]

As can be seen in the writings of theologian Muhammad al-Tijani (b. A. D. 1943), "Both Sunni and Shi'a groups agree all along with regard to the importance of the Qur'an and of the Sunnah, accepting them as the bases upon which they establish the implementation of their faith."[11] Where the two major Muslim sects disagree is not concerning the Sunnah or the Qur'an, but rather the Imamate. The Sunni Imam is a temporary spiritual leader that is nominated by the Muslim community, whereas the Shi'a Imam is often regarded as a messiah who can perform miracles.[12] It should go without saying that there are exceptions; such as in the case with some Sunni scholars believing in the continued existence of Imam Mahdi, which is primarily a Shi'a belief. A few of which include Al-Bayhaqi (d. A. D. 1066), Fakhr al-Din al-Razi (d. A. D. 1209), and Ali ibn al-Athir (d. A. D. 1233), not to mention all the scholars listed in *The Promised Savior*.[13]

---

[8] *"The Shi'a of India"* Ch. 1, p. 3.

[9] The Sunna(h) is comprised of the traditional sayings, actions, etc. of the Holy Prophet Muhammad. Its importance is near that of the Qur'an.

[10] *"The Shi'a of India"* Ch. 1, p. 4.

[11] *"The Shia: The Real Followers of the Sunnah"* Ch. 1, p. 2.

[12] *"Islam"* Trans. Halide Edib, p. 185.

[13] "The Promised Savior" p. 28.

The Shi'a account of al-Mahdi's heritage begins with the father of Muhammad al-Mahdi and goes all the way back to the Holy Prophet Muhammad. Muhammad al-Mahdi was born in A. D. 869, which means that if he were still alive to this day, as some believe, he would be over 1,100 years old.

Muhammad al-Mahdi's father was Hasan al-Askari (d. A. D. 874), the eleventh Imam. The father of Hasan al-Askari was Ali al-Hadi (d. A. D. 868), the tenth Imam, and the father of Ali al-Hadi was Muhammad al-Jawad (d. A. D. 835), the ninth Imam. The father of Muhammad al-Jawad was Ali al-Ridha (d. A. D. 819), the eighth Imam, and the father of Ali al-Ridha was Musa al-Kadhim (d. A. D. 799), the seventh Imam. The father of Musa al-Kadhim was Ja'far al-Sadiq (d. A. D. 765), the sixth Imam, and the father of Ja'far al-Sadiq was Muhammad al-Baqir (d. A. D. 743), the fifth Imam. The father of Muhammad al-Baqir was Ali ibn Husayn Zayn al-Abidin (d. A. D. 713), the fourth Imam, and the father of Ali ibn Husayn Zayn al-Abidin was Husayn ibn Ali (d. A. D. 680), the third Imam. Husayn ibn Ali was then the son of Fatimah Bint Muhammad, wife of Imam Ali (d. A. D. 661) and daughter of the Holy Prophet Muhammad. What this concludes is that Muhammad al-Mahdi is the tenth-generation grandson of the Holy Prophet Muhammad.

This family history is supported by the writings of the Muslim scholar Al-Daraqutni (d. A. D. 995) where Al-Daraqutni records that the Holy Prophet Muhammad placed his arm on the shoulder of Husayn ibn Ali, the eight-generation grandfather of Imam Mahdi and told him that the Mahdi would come from his progeny.[14]

Ibn Majah[15] (d. A. D. 887) believed that Jesus Christ was the Mahdi/Messiah that Muhammad referred to when speaking of a messianic figure that would appear/reappear at

---

[14] "The Promised Savior" p. 27.

[15] Ibid p. 30.

the end of time. This is an unpopular argument given that both major Muslim sects agree that Jesus Christ will descend from heaven to follow Imam Mahdi in prayer. One account states that Jesus will descend in the morning at a white minaret in Damascus, Syria, where he will ask Imam Mahdi to lead the prayer for the Muslims. Other accounts suggest a descent in Mecca, Jerusalem, or India.[16] Regardless of where this descent is to take place, it goes without debate that Jesus Christ (Isa) and Muhammad al-Mahdi are separate individuals. They merely share the same objective.

Another perspective worth noting regarding the birth of Imam Mahdi is that he was born of the offspring of Hasan ibn Ali (d. A. D. 670), the second Imam, rather than of the progeny of Husayn ibn Ali (d. A. D. 680), the third Imam. This is another unpopular view but has been argued by the Muslim scholar Abu Ishaq Shami (d. A. D. 940). The argument of Imam Mahdi being born of Hasan instead of Husain could be the result of a simple spelling error.

Polymath Taftazani[17] (d. A. D. 1390) and theologian Ibn Taymiyyah (d. A. D. 1328) were both of the opinion that Imam Mahdi's time had passed. In Ibn Taymiyyah's book titled *Minhaj as-Sunnah an-Nabawiyyah*, Shia Muslims are compared to idol worshippers for their firm attachment to Imam Mahdi. Among the Abrahamic religions, idolatry is frowned upon, because it suggests the worship of something other than God as God. Calling Shias idol worshippers solidified Taymiyyah's stance against them. If al-Mahdi had already come and gone, then Taymiyyah saw no reason to hold al-Mahdi is such high esteem.

A potential fault in this opinion held by Taftazani and Taymiyyah is that it may disagree with a prophetic saying that states 'He who dies without knowing the Imam of his time,

---

[16] "Darurat-ul-Islam" p. 40-41.

[17] "The Awaited Savior" p. 39.

dies the death of ignorance.' Ibn Ḥajar al-ʿAsqalānī (d. A. D. 1449) and Sunni Islamic scholar Aḥmad ibn Muḥammad Qasṭallānī[18] (d. A. D. 1517) have been known to disagree with Taymiyyah in this regard.

Some scholars have also argued that Hasan al-Askari (d. A. D. 874), commonly believed to be the father of Imam Mahdi, never had a child, leading many to believe that Hasan al-Askari was the Mahdi himself.[19] Muhammad ibn Jarir al-Tabari (d. A. D. 923) is among those who held this belief.

Further complicating the issue of al-Mahdi's birth and personage are accounts of Ja'far al-Sadiq (d. A. D. 765), the sixth Imam. Sadiq heard the Holy Prophet Muhammad say that any who deny Mahdi of His (Holy Prophet Muhammad's) offspring shall die a death of ignorance. So here we have a subject that Muslims from both major sects agree upon, that there will be a Mahdi who will appear/reappear at the end of time, but the details regarding the identity of this Mahdi cannot be agreed on.

Ja'far al-Sadiq, quoting the Holy Prophet Muhammad, says that any who obey Mahdi obeys Him (Holy Prophet Muhammad) and any who deny Mahdi deny Him. The Holy Prophet Muhammad then states that he will complain before Allah about those who reject what He says about the Mahdi. This further testifies to the point of why Imam Mahdi is not someone who can simply be ignored. Whether we understand who he is as an individual or not, all Muslims must respect him, whoever al-Mahdi may be. Ja'far al-Sadiq has also said that the occultation, or time spent in hiding, of Imam Mahdi will be so long that many will begin to doubt his existence. This supports the argument of why many believe in the continued existence of al-Mahdi despite his

---

[18] The opinions of Al-Qasṭallānī are recorded in his book titled *al-Mawahib al-Ladunniyyah*.

[19] "The Promised Savior" p. 10.

birth having been over 1,100 years ago.[20]

For those who are not followers of the Islamic Faith, it may be hard to understand how so many people could accept the idea of someone living for 1,100+ years. This is not the only account of its kind. There are other instances in Islam where people are granted exceptionally long lives. According to many Islamic traditions, Allah has gifted multiple people with long lives, such as Noah, Khidr, and Isa. Some Sunnis believe in the continued life of Dajjal (the Antichrist) as well. In his book *To Be with the Truthful*, Muslim scholar/theologian Muhammad al-Tijani (born A. D. 1943) explains why Muslims should not have a problem with the idea of al-Mahdi's continued existence by giving many examples of similar instances found within the Qur'an.[21] A few examples include Allah having brought 'Uzayr (Ezra) back to life after one hundred years, and how al-Khidr[22] and Iblis[23] are thought to still be alive as well. Muhammad al-Tijani also takes the route of explaining the belief in miracles in general; such as the parting of the Red Sea for Moses and the Children of Israel, or how Lord Abraham avoided getting

---

[20] "The Promised Savior" p. 43.

[21] "*Li-'Akuna Ma 'Al Sadiqin*" p. 216-217.

[22] In the Qur'an, al-Khidr is merely referred to as 'One of Our servants' but Tradition pens this 'servant' as having been al-Khidr. He has been described as a mysterious being who holds the secrets to some of life's paradoxes. By looking at Ch. 18 of the *Holy Qur'an* titled *Al-Kahf* we can see that even the Prophet Moses seeks information from al-Khidr. Beginning with section 9 of Ch. 18, verse 66; "Moses said to him [al-Khidr]: may I follow thee, on the footing that thou teach me something of the (Higher) Truth which thou hast been taught?" continuing with this dialogue in section 9 we pick up at verse 70 where al-Khidr is responding to the request of Moses; "If then thou wouldst follow me, ask me no questions about anything until I myself speak to thee concerning it."

[23] Iblis (Satan) is often regarded as a Jinn or leader of the Jinn (demons of good and evil), and according to *An Encyclopedia of Religions* by Maurice A. Canney, the Jinn were created from fire. Beginning with section 4 Ch. 2 of *The Holy Qur'an* titled *Al-Baqarah* we see mention of Iblis in reference to Adam from the Garden of Eden. Starting with verse 34 "And behold, We said to the angels: 'Bow down to Adam:' and they bowed down: Not so Iblis: he refused and was haughty: He was of those who rejected Faith."

burned by flames because Allah cooled the flames in an act of protection.[24]

The final point to be addressed by Muhammad al-Tijani in defense of al-Mahdi's continued existence is that there are grand tombs/shrines dedicated to the other Imams, but that there has not yet been one erected for Imam Mahdi[25]. To this point, as will be discussed in Chapter IV, there are tombs dedicated to those who have claimed to be Imam Mahdi, but the majority do not recognize their Mahdiship. Sunni scholar Ibn Arabi (d. A. D. 1240), scholar Sibt ibn al-Jawzi (d. A. D. 1256), Ibn al-Khashshab (d. A. D. 1125), Persian Islamic scholar Muhammad al-Bukhari Hanafi (d. A. D. 870), and historian Al-Baladhuri (d. A. D. 892) have also defended the continued life of Imam Mahdi.[26]

Disagreement among religious beliefs is not only present between adherents of different religions but is also prevalent among people sharing the same religion. The importance of al-Mahdi is debated among Muslim sects, with some regarding him very highly, others respecting what he had done, and some believing he has not even shown himself yet. Some Muslims, such as Iranian Sunni philosopher Fakhr al-Din al-Razi (d. A. D. 1209), theologian Ibn Taymiyyah, and polymath Taftazani (d. A. D. 1390)[27] believe that no one can benefit from seeking the Mahdi, because we simply do not know enough about him.

---

[24] *"Li- 'Akuna Ma 'Al Sadiqin"* p. 216-217.

[25] Ibid p. 217.

[26] "The Promised Savior" p. 28-29.

[27] "The Promised Savior" p. 40.

# III
# IF HE IS ALIVE, WHERE IS HE?

If Imam Mahdi has already been born and continues to live to this day, then the question remains; where is he? Although the answer is elusive, there are many locations worth noting. An understanding commonly accepted by those who believe in his continued life is that he resides in isolation, such as on an island or in a cave.

One hiding place thought to house Imam Mahdi is an island known as Khadra Island[28], but nowadays it may go by a different name. Khadra Island is often referred to as Green Island, but there are multiple islands that share this name. One is in the Red Sea, another is off the coast of Queensland, Australia, and the third is off the coast of Tanzania, South America, nowadays referred to as Pemba Island.

The Green Island of the Red Sea initially sounds promising, given its proximity to Islam's founding place of Saudi Arabia, but it was man-made less than one-hundred years ago during

---

[28] "The Promised Savior" p. 45.

World War II. The other Green Islands make much less sense geographically and are not devoid of people, so if Imam Mahdi were to reside on one of them it may be hard for him to remain hidden.

The writings of Ibn Taymiyyah (d. A. D. 1328) aid in this next location, as he once stated that many Shia Muslims believe his residence to be a basement located in [Samarra], Iraq.[29] In *The Promised Savior*, one passage reads; "They [Shi'as] sometimes put animals such as mule, horse, etc. over there [near the Samarra basement] so that the awaited Imam [& Isa] would ride on them after reappearing. They commissioned a person to stand by the basement and keep calling on [the] awaited Mahdi to reappear."[30] What is intriguing about this account is that the details are very similar to those given regarding a basement in Hillah, Iraq. Some sources state that this was the last place Mahdi had been seen and thus it was given the name 'the sanctuary of the Master of the Hour.'[31] The account of this location in Hillah states that a horse was led to the sanctuary and the horsemen cried out to the Mahdi, asking him to come forth.[32] Ibn Khaldun (d. A. D. 1406) also commented on this sanctuary located in Hillah, but in his comments he refers to Imam Mahdi as Muhammad bin Hasan Askari[33], father of Muhammad al-Mahdi, and the sanctuary, in this case, is

---

[29] "In his *Minhaj al-Sunna*, Ibn Taymiyyah [...] commenting on Shias' belief in Imam Mahdi, says very rudely: 'One of the stupid acts done by Shias is that they have devoted to awaited Mahdi particular places where they keep waiting for him. The basement (sardab) of [Samarra] considered by Shias as a place where Mahdi has disappeared is among such locations.'" (The Promised Savior) p. 8.

[30] Ibid p. 8.

[31] "*The Mahdi: Past and Present*" p. 41-42.

[32] Ibid p. 41-42.

[33] "The Promised Savior" p. 45.

22

believed to be his father's house/basement.[34]

In an account from Isfahan, Iran, in the 1500s, states that al-Mahdi is thought to be hidden in a palace;
"In their palace at [Isfahan] the Sufis[35] always kept two horses magnificently harnessed ready to receive him [Mahdi] when he should deign to take once more the reins of government. One of these horses was for the Mahdi, the other for his lieutenant, Jesus Christ."[36]

Looking back to the time of Muhammad ibn al-Hanafiyyah (d. A. D. 700), son of Imam Ali (d. A. D. 661), one can find another location thought to be the residence of Imam Mahdi. Muhammad ibn al-Hanafiyyah had a claim to Mahdiship over one-hundred years before the birth of Muhammad al-Mahdi, son of Hasan al-Askari (d. A. D. 874). Among those who supported the Mahdiship of Hanafiyyah include poet Kuthayyir (d. A. D. 723) and poet Sayyid al-Ḥimyarī (d. A. D. 789). Both of these poets have claimed that Hanafiyyah had not died but that he remained hiding at Mount Radwa, a mountain of western Saudi Arabia.[37] One account states; "The poet sang that he [Mahdi] was hidden for a time near Medina, in the valley of Radwa, where water and honey flow."[38] Not long after the death or disappearance of Muhamad ibn al-Hanafiyyah is the birth of Muhammad al-Nafs al-Zakiyya (d. A. D. 762), who is then also labeled the Mahdi, as a young child. Following the death of Muhammad al-Nafs al-Zakiyya, at the age of forty-four, his followers

---

[34] Quoting Ibn Khaldun (d. A. D. 1406) – "Shias think that their twelfth Imam – Muhammad bin Hasan Askari called Mahdi – has gone into hiding in the basement of his father's house in [Hillah], after he and his mother were arrested." (Ibid) p. 45.

[35] The term Sufi refers to the followers of Sufism, Muslims who "devoted themselves to a life of devotion and seclusion." One of their main doctrines states that "the Spirit of God is in all he has made" and that to love him is the only real thing, whereas everything else is a mere illusion. (*An Encyclopedia of Religions*) p. 337.

[36] *"The Mahdi: Past and Present"* p. 42-43.

[37] *"Islamic Messianism"* p. 11.

[38] *"The Mahdi: Past and Present"* p. 30-31.

maintained that he had not died but rather had been hiding in one of the hills found on the way to Mecca from Najd.[39]

If Imam Mahdi is in hiding, then it is no wonder he has remained hidden, because nobody knows where to look. He resides on either the elusive island of Khadra, a basement in Iraq, a palace in Iran, or the mountains of Saudi Arabia. Considering that many have claimed to be the promised Mahdi throughout history, there are numerous opinions on where he can be found. These opinions are often contradictory.

---

[39] *"Islamic Messianism"* p. 11.

# IV
# HISTORICAL MAHDIS

To speak on al-Mahdi without mentioning the Mahdis of history, those who have claimed to be him, would be incomplete. As previously discussed, al-Mahdi is expected to appear/reappear at the end of time. Upon making his presence known, he will bring justice and eliminate evil throughout the world. To die before having accomplished this objective often leads to the Mahdi claimant being labeled a false prophet. Here are a few of their stories.

## Muhammad Jaunpuri (A. D. 1443 – 1505)

Muhammad Jaunpuri, born in Janupur, India is said to have taken on the role of a "saint *walī*"[40] in the year 1465 which soon brought him followers from Janupur and Mecca.[41] These followers were described as "converted Hindus and foreign Musalmáns [Muslims]"[42]. Muhammad Jaunpuri became recognized as the leader of the Mahdavi order and his followers were known as Mahdavis. At the age of 52 in the year 1495, Muhammad Jaunpuri performed Hajj, a Muslim tradition of going off on a pilgrimage to the holy city of Mecca. While in Mecca he made his claim to Mahdiship.[43] It was not long after that he was asked to leave. Many Muslims had consulted scholar Al-Suyuti (d. A. D. 1505) regarding Jaunpuri's claim to Mahdiship and Al-Suyuti did not offer the recognition Jaunpuri needed. Al-Suyuti felt it was not yet time for the Mahdi to appear, and he was not the only one to hold this opinion. Abu'l-Fazl ibn Mubarak (d. A. D. 1602) had also denied Jaunpuri's claim, but he did respect him as a scholar and mystic.[44]

Upon being asked to leave, Muhammad Jaunpuri left, heading back to India where he stopped through Ahmedabad in the year 1497. Following his visit in Ahmedabad, Muhammad Jaunpuri stopped through the town of Pattan in 1499, where he made his claim of Mahdiship once again.[45] During his stay in Ahmedabad, he crossed paths with a

---

[40] "Such a saint if no miracles appear through him [the Wali], is not a true Wali." (*An Encyclopedia of Religions*) p. 381.

[41] "Muhammad [Jaunpuri] at the age of forty began to act as a saint *walī*, and both at Janupur and afterwards at [Mecca], drew around him a large body of followers." (*Gazetteer of the Bombay Presidency*) p. 62.

[42] Ibid p. 62.

[43] "Bada'uni [likely historian 'Abd al-Qadir Bada'uni who died in A. D. 1615] said that Sayyid Muhammad Jaunpuri declared himself the Mahdi when he reached Mecca." (*The Millennial Sovereign*) p. 159.

[44] Ibid. p. 290.

[45] "*Gazetteer of the Bombay Presidency*" p. 62.

young man who had been quarreling with a lover. The story goes that Muhammad Jaunpuri, followed by some of his adherents, were on their way to the Sabarmati River for their morning devotions. As they crossed paths with this young man, Muhammad Jaunpuri says, "I can show the way to the Divine Love, to him who has come away in anger from his Worldly Love." After hearing these words, the young man screamed, grew faint, and soon became an ardent follower of Jaunpuri.[46]

The movements of Jaunpuri then continue onward through India, where he attracted more followers while stopping through Gujarat and Ahmednagar. Mahmud Begada of Gujarat (d. A. D. 1511) and Malik Ahmad Nizam Shah I (d. A.D. 1510) had a lot of respect for Jaunpuri, but Sultan Mahmud Begada's respect waned and he ultimately expelled Jaunpuri from the area.[47] Following his expulsion, Muhammad Jaunpuri arrived in Farah, Afghanistan, where he met his death, likely by fever, at the age of 62. The cause of death is not accepted by all, because some believe he was murdered.

Upon Jaunpuri's death, the Mahdavis maintained that he was the promised Mahdi and then parted ways with some following Jaunpuri's companion Sayad Khondmir (d. A. D. 1524) and others following Jaunpuri's companion Sayad Muhammad.[48] Those who chose to follow Sayad Khondmir went forth to Gujarat, India, and those who chose to remain with Sayad Muhammad remained in Farah, Afghanistan. The Mahdavis who went to Gujarat practiced their faith openly and grew in number until 1523. At this time, they were at odds with Shams-ud-Din Muzaffar Shah II, ruler of the Muzaffarid dynasty. He had many of them

---

[46] This account has been recorded in the *Gazetteer of the Bombay Presidency* (p. 63), and from this same source, it states that the account has been recorded in the *Mirât-i-Sikandari*.

[47] "*Writings of the Mughal World*" p. 174.

[48] "*Gazetteer of the Bombay Presidency*" p. 63.

killed. The Mahdavis tried to fight back but were defeated nonetheless, along with Sayed Khondmir.

In 1645, the Mahdavis were at odds with Emperor Aurangzeb (d. A.D. 1707), ruler of the Mughal Empire.[49] They were killed for their belief that the Mahdi had already come and gone.

Muhammad Jaunpuri was said to perform miracles such as bringing life to the dead, sight to the blind, and speech to the dumb. These miracles are common among messianic/prophetic individuals.

A tomb was erected in his name, often simply referred to as the Tomb of Muhammad Jaunpuri, and it can be found in Farah, Afghanistan, the city where his life had come to an end.

---

[49] Ibid p. 63.

## Siyyid `Alí Muḥammad Shírází (A. D. 1819 – 1850)

The claim to Mahdiship of Siyyid `Alí Muḥammad Shírází is an interesting one considering that he was the founder of Bábism, which later led to the founding of the Bahá'í Faith, a faith that has millions of followers. To begin, I would like to refer to a quote found within *The Dawn-Breakers*, possibly one of the most notable texts written on the early days of Bábism, which goes to show how the Báb's claim to Mahdiship was a bit different from those of the past.

"He made himself known as the Qá'im, the High Prophet or Messiah so long promised, so eagerly expected by the Muḥammadan world. He added to this the declaration that he was also the Gate (that is, the Báb) through whom a greater Manifestation than Himself was to enter the human realm."[50]

A better understanding as to what the Qá'im is can be seen through further reading of *The Dawn-Breakers* where the Qá'im is described by way of comparison to the Mahdi and Isa which has been included below.

"The shí'ahs look for the Qá'im, who is to come in the fullness of time, and for the return of the Imám Husayn. The sunnís await the appearance of the [Mahdi] and 'the return of Jesus Christ [Isa]."[51]

This explains that the Qá'im is essentially the equivalent of the Mahdi, as they are both regarded as a messiah. The 'greater manifestation' that is to enter through the Báb is Bahá'u'lláh (d. A. D. 1892), founder of the Bahá'í Faith.

---

[50] "*The Dawn-Breakers*" p. 20.

[51] Ibid p. 21.

Before moving on to the series of events that form the Báb's life, there are a few key things that must first be noted. The Báb's movement began as a branch of the Shi'a sect of Islam, and the idea of a Gate came about around the disappearance of Muhammad al-Mahdi, son of Hasan al-Askari. This disappearance occurred around A.D. 873. When Muhammad al-Mahdi went into hiding, he still communicated with his followers, but did so through an intermediary. The intermediary was known as the 'Gate'.[52]

Born in Shiraz, Iran the Báb was raised by his uncle, Áqá Siyyid 'Alí, due to his father's early passing. Although he was not given an opportunity to spend much time with his father, he would still manage to follow in his footsteps when it came to choosing a profession, which meant that he would go on to become a merchant.[53]

In time the Báb would go on to share his book known as the *Persian Bayán* or *The Báb's Bayán*, which became one of the central texts of Bábism. The problem with presenting the contents of his declaration, as stated in the *Persian Bayán*, is that it suggested a new religious law, which brought forth the opposition of the priestly figures of that time. He was quickly seen as "an enemy of sound learning, a subverter of Islám, a traitor to Muḥammad, and a peril not only to the holy church but the social order and to the State itself."[54]

On the other hand, we find much praise for the Báb, with one of many examples found in *The Dawn-Breakers* stating:

"[A]fter His Declaration He quickly became in Persia a widely popular figure. He would win over almost all with whom He was brought into personal contact with, often converting His gaolers [jailers] to His Faith and turning the

---

[52] *"The Dawn-Breakers"* p. 21.

[53] Ibid. p. 74. Original sourced credited to A. L. M. Nicholas in *Siyyid 'Alí-Muḥammad dit le Báb* p. 189.

[54] *"The Dawn-Breakers"* p. 21.

ill-disposed into admiring friends."[55]

What can be gleaned from these two accounts is that although the priestly figures and State authorities abhorred the Báb 's declaration, there were still many people who came to regard themselves as Bábís, which may have been a dangerous position. Showing support for the Báb opened them up to accusations of disloyalty to the government, given its stance on religious law.[56] Evidence of this can be seen in the many episodes that occurred during the early days of Bábism where the Bábís were persecuted and in some cases where they even fought back, such as the events that unfolded in Mazandaran, Nayriz, and Zanjan.

In the year 1844, at the age of twenty-five, Siyyid `Alí Muḥammad Shírází made his declaration that became the starting point for the Bábí Movement.[57] Among the first to believe in his words was that of Siyyid Kázim[58] (d. A. D. 1843), leading figure of Shaykhism at the time, who was also the son of Shaykh Ahmad (d. A. D. 1826), founder of the Shaykhism movement. Given that Siyyid Kázim recognized the mission of Siyyid `Alí Muḥammad Shírází, many of the

---

[55] Ibid p. 23.

[56] "The bigotry of the Muḥammadans from the Sháh downwards could be readily roused against any religious development. The Bábís could be accused of disloyalty to the Sháh, and dark political motives could be attributed to their activities." (*The Dawn-Breakers*) p. 23.

[57] "The author [of *The Dawn-Breakers*] was thirteen years old when the Báb declared Himself, having been born in the village of Zarand in Persia on the eighteenth day of Safar, 1247 A. H. [July 29th of 1831]." (Ibid) p. 25.

[58] "*The Dawn-Breakers*" footnote, p. 49. The resting place of Siyyid Kázim is pictured as well, minus the tombstone. "His sacred remains were interred within the precincts of the shrine of Imám Ḥusayn. [...] "He was buried behind the window in the corridor of the tomb of the Lord of Confessors. The tomb was built on an incline toward the interior of the forbidden precincts." [*The Dawn-Breakers* p. 62.] The source of the footnote lends credit to A. L. M. Nicholas in *Essai sur le Shaykhisme*, p. 31.

Shaykhís converted to Bábís upon Siyyid Kázim's demise.[59]
Mullá Husayn (d. A. D. 1849), a disciple of Siyyid Kázim,
inquired upon his fellow disciples as to why they had
remained stationary when Siyyid Kázim wanted them to
"[Q]uit their homes, scatter far and wide, purge their hearts
from every idle desire, and dedicate themselves to the quest
of Him to whose advent he had so often alluded."[60] Upon
being questioned on this, the fellow followers openly stated
that if he, Mullá Husayn, were to claim that he was the
promised one they would all believe in him without
question.[61] Mullá Husayn denied being the promised one.

Mullá Husayn undertook the task of scattering in search of
'Him,' the Báb, who he, Siyyid Kázim, had so often alluded
to. While on his journey, he ran into the Báb, unaware that
he was the one who he had been looking for. The Báb made
a good impression through his hospitality, but upon making
his claim of being the promised one, Mullá Husayn remained
hesitant. *The Dawn-Breakers* included a picture of the room
they shared when the Báb made his declaration.

To prove himself, the Báb was asked to "reveal, without
the least hesitation or reflection, a commentary on the Súrih
of Joseph[62], in a style and language entirely different from the

---

[59] "[A]fter the death of Siyyid Kázim-i-Rashtí, it [Shaykhism] became divided into
two branches. One branch under the name of Bábism, flowered as foreshadowed by
the strength of the movement created by Shaykh Aḥmad [...] The other, under the
leadership of Karím Khán-i-Qájár-i-Kirmání, will continue its struggles against the
Shí'ite sect [...]" (*The Dawn-Breakers*) footnote, p. 63. The source is credited to A. L.
M. Nicholas in *Essai sur le Shaykhisme*, Ch. II, p. 31.

[60] "*The Dawn-Breakers*" p. 63.

[61] "'[If] you [Mullá Husayn] claim to be the promised One, we shall all readily and
unquestionably submit. We herein pledge our loyalty and obedience to whatever you
bid us perform." To which Mullá Husayn responds, "God forbid!"" (Ibid) p. 63.

[62] Ibid, p. 67. The Súrih of Joseph corresponds with chapter 12 of *The Holy Qur'an*
titled *Yúsuf*. "The story is similar to but not identical with the Biblical story [...]"
(*The Holy Qur-an: English translation of the meanings and Commentary*) p. 621. This is
referring to the story of Joseph that can be found starting in chapter 30 of the first
book in the Old Testament of the *Holy Bible* titled *Genesis*.

prevailing standards of the time." Siyyid Kázim was unable to do this, which would make for an awe-inspiring feat, and even more so considering that the Báb was not particularly known for his intelligence, given how little he attended school. This commentary on the Súrih of Joseph came to be known as *Qayyúmu'l-Asmá*.[63] The rate at which the Báb was able to write this commentary very much impressed Mullá Husayn as can be seen here where, after observing, he stated: "He took up his pen and with incredible rapidity revealed the entire Súrih of Mulk, the first chapter of His commentary on the Súrih of Joseph [...] Not for once did He interrupt the flow of verses which streamed from His pen. Not once did He pause till the Súrih of Mulk was finished."[64] After revealing each verse of this commentary, the Báb would recite verses 180-182 from Súrih 37 of the Holy Qur'an titled *Aṣ-Ṣáffát*.[65] At this time the Báb referred to himself as the Gate of God and to Mullá Husayn as Bábu'l-Báb, the gate to the Gate of God.

Following this conversation between Mullá Husayn and the Báb, Mullá Husayn was once again presented with the belief that he himself was the promised Qá'i. Accounts of this instance state that it occurred at the Masjid-i-Ílkhání. A man known as Mullá 'Alí, alongside his companions, stated:

"We bear you such loyalty that if you should claim to be the promised Qá'im we would all unhesitatingly submit. [...] We

---

[63] Excerpts are included in *Selections from the Writings of the Báb*, found in the Bahá'í Reference Library.

[64] *"The Dawn-Breakers"* p. 67.

[65] "Far from the glory of thy Lord, the All-Glorious, be that which His creatures affirm of Him! And peace be upon His Messengers! And praise be to God, the Lord of all beings!" (Ibid) p. 68-69. A variance in the wording of these verses can be found in *The Holy Qur-an: English translation of the meanings and Commentary* where it reads as:
"Glory to thy Lord, The lord of Honor And Power (He is free) from what they ascribe (To Him)! And Peace on the messengers! And Praise to Allah, The Lord and Cherisher Of the Worlds." p. 1368.

have followed you to this place, ready to acknowledge whomsoever you accept, in the hope of seeking the shelter of His protection and of passing successfully through the tumult and agitation that must needs signalize the last Hour."[66]

Mullá Husayn brushed off being the promised Qá'im and did not disclose that he knew the man they were looking for. Later that same night, Mullá Husayn would find, to his surprise, that this same man he had turned away had found his way to his doorstep. He claimed that God led him there through a dream. The next morning, they went to visit the Báb where their arrival had already been anticipated.[67] In the previous encounter of Mullá 'Alí and Mullá Husayn, Alí was accompanied by twelve others. With time, each of these twelve came to the same realization as 'Alí on their own accord. For some, the realization occurred during prayer and for others it occurred in their sleep. All of them become followers of the Báb, forming the first thirteen Letters of the Living, best described as the Apostles of the Báb.[68] The first eighteen followers of the Báb formed the Eighteen Letters of the Living.[69] Of these eighteen 'souls' one of them was to

---

[66] *"The Dawn-Breakers"* p. 70.

[67] Ibid p. 71.

[68] Ibid. 71-72. The Eighteen letters of the Living: Mullá Ḥusayn-i-Bushrú'í (Mullá Husayn), Muḥammad Ḥasan (His brother), Muḥammad-Báqir (His nephew), Mullá 'Alíy-i-Bastámí, Mullá Khudá-Bakhsh-i-Quchání (Mullá 'Alí), Mullá Ḥasan-i-Bajistání, Siyyid Ḥusayn-i-Yazdí, Mírzá Muḥammad Rawdíh-Khán-i-Yazdí, Sa'íd-i-Hindí, Mullá Maḥmúd-i-Khú'í, Mullá Jalíl-i-Urúmí, Mullá Aḥmad-i-Ibdal-i-Marághi'í, Mullá Báqir-i-Tabrízí, Mullá Yusif-i-Ardibílí, Mírzá Hádí (Son of Mullá 'Abdu'l-Vahháb-i-Qazvíní), Mírzá Muḥammad-i 'Alíy-i-Qazvíní, Táhirih, & Quddús. The Báb himself is sometimes referred to as the nineteenth Letter of the Living, as is Bahá'u'lláh regarded as the twentieth. *"The Dawn-Breakers"* p. 13 & 77.

[69] "Eighteen souls must, in the beginning, spontaneously and of their own accord, accept Me and recognize the truth of my Revelation. Unwarned and uninvited, each of these must seek independently to find Me. And when their number is complete, one of them must needs be chosen to accompany Me on My pilgrimage to Mecca and Medina. [...] We shall instruct them to teach the Word of God and to quicken the souls of men." - Báb (*The Dawn-Breakers*) p. 69.

accompany the Báb to Mecca and Medina where he would deliver the message of God.

What of the Báb's personal life? At the age of twenty-two he married the sister of Mírzá Siyyid Ḥasan and Mírzá Abu'l Qásim. In his commentary on the Súrih of Joseph (Súrih of Qarabat), the Báb refers to her as Sárá where he goes on to say, "In truth I have taken the angles of heaven and those who dwell in Paradise as witnesses of our betrothal."[70] A son followed this marriage between Siyyid `Alí Muḥammad Shírází and Sárá. He was named Aḥmad. The Báb would live to see the death of his only son, unfortunately, which occurred in the year 1843 A. D. This was the same year he was born. His resting place is marked by a single tree in Shiraz, Iran.[71]

Following the Báb 's proclamation, Mullá 'Alí, the fifth Letter of the Living, was sent on a mission by the Báb, where, in Najaf, Iraq he announced the Báb's mission. This brought 'Alí many oppressors. During his announcement of the Báb's mission, Mullá 'Alí said:

"From the pen of this unschooled Háshimite Youth of Persia there have streamed, within the space of forty-eight hours, as great a number of verses, of prayers, of homilies, and scientific treatises, as would equal in volume the whole of the Qur'án, which it took Muḥammad, the Prophet of God, twenty-three years to reveal!"[72] Mullá 'Alí was later in chains and was considered "[A] wrecker of Islám, a calumniator of the Prophet, an instigator of mischief, a

---

[70] Ibid p. 74. Footnote credits A. L. M. Nicholas with the translation of the passage regarding the Báb's marriage.

[71] Ibid 73-75.

[72] Ibid p. 83.

disgrace to the Faith, and worthy of the penalty of death."[73]
He was then placed in a prison of Baghdad. Details of his life
after imprisonment are not well documented but he had
grown ill and likely died while being moved to
Constantinople.

Meanwhile, Siyyid `Alí Muhammad Shírází was addressing
the other Letters of the Living where he explained why they
should come out triumphant in their act of spreading the
word of God. In so doing, he refers to multiple accounts that
are present in the Qur'an that, in his belief, give weight to his
argument.

"Has He [Allah] not, in past days, caused Abraham, in spite
of his seeming helplessness, to triumph over the forces of
Nimrod? Has He not enabled Moses, whose staff was His
only companion, to vanquish Pharaoh and his hosts? Has he
not established the ascendancy of Jesus, poor and lowly as
He was in the eyes of men, over the combined forces of the
Jewish people? Has he not subjected the barbarous and
militant tribes of Arabia to the holy and transforming
discipline of Muhammad, His Prophet? Arise in His name,
put your trust wholly in Him, and be assured of ultimate
victory."[74]

The Báb's statement regarding Abraham is likely concerning
Súrih 2 of the Holy Qur'an titled *Al-Baqarah* where in section
35 beginning with verse 258 we see Abraham in
disagreement with someone, often believed to be king
Nimrod. An argument between the two ensues regarding
how Allah 'giveth life and death' where Nimrod proceeds to
respond with a barbaric display of power where he shows
how he can give life and take it as well. Abraham counters by

---

[73] Ibid p. 84.

[74] *"The Dawn-Breakers"* p. 85-86.

saying "But it is Allah that causeth the sun to rise from the East: Do thou then cause it to rise from the West."[75] Nimrod was outraged because he was unable to display this sort of power.

In the story of Moses and Pharaoh, found in Section 13 of Súrih 7 of the *Holy Qur'an* titled *Al-A'ráf* beginning with verse 103 it states:

"Then after them We sent Moses with Our Signs to Pharaoh and his chiefs."

Instead of being killed, Moses was pitted against men of magic, which was essentially a battle of magic trickery to see who would gather the praise of the onlookers. When asked, Moses chose to allow the men of magic to perform first and as they proceeded he threw his rod to intercept the illusion they had been fooling the onlookers with, thus bringing to light their deception.
"So when they threw, they bewitched the eyes of the people, and struck terror into them: and they showed a great (feat of magic). We revealed to Moses "Throw thy rod": and behold! It swallows up all the falsehoods which they fake! Thus the truth was confirmed. And all that they did was made of no effect. So they were vanquished there and then, and turned about humble. But the sorcerers fell down prostrate in adoration. Saying "We believe in the Lord of the Worlds""[76]

The Báb's reference to the ascendancy of Jesus is supported by Súrih 3, section 6, verse 55 of the Holy Qur'an where Allah says "O Jesus! I will take thee and raise thee to Myself and clear thee (of the falsehoods) [...]" As stated in a

---

[75] "*The Holy Qur-an: English translation of the meaning and Commentary*" Verse 258 from Súrih 2 titled *Al-Baqarah*. The story of Ibrahim/Abraham can be found in Súrih 19 titled *Maryam* beginning with verse 41.

[76] Ibid, Súrih 7 titled *Al-A'raf*, section 14, verses 115-121.

commentary on this same verse we are told that "The guilt of the Jews remained, but Jesus was eventually taken up to Allah."[77]

The Báb had also decided to do something a bit out of the ordinary, though for a good reason, and that was to instruct the Letters of the Living to record the names of all who accepted the faith as well as those who had denied it. He intended to record the names of those who accepted the faith in the Tablet of God.[78] This may have also been a tactic used by the Báb to ensure the continuation of the faith, which in October of 1844 was assured as he read the letter sent to him from Mullá Husayn. In this letter, Husayn detailed the accounts of his journey and described to what extent the faith was being accepted.[79] Shortly after enjoying such reassurance, the Báb began his journey to Mecca and Medina through Shiraz, Iran and by route of the Persian Gulf. His journey took two months' time, a moment of which was not spent being idle, regardless of unforgiving sailing conditions. His companions on this journey were Quddús, the most recent addition to the Letters of the Living, and the Báb's trusted Ethiopian servant who never left his side.[80] The journey that followed was an arduous one by camel and foot. During the journey, the Báb was robbed of his writings and he performed a lamb sacrifice. Many of his writings were stolen while he was attending to his morning prayer, and although he could have seen this as an unfortunate setback, he chose to believe that this thief would bring his writings to places they would not have otherwise gone, spreading the word of God by chance and so he was content. While approaching Mecca from the east, the Báb

---

[77] *"The Holy Qur-an: English translation of the meaning and Commentary"* p. 156.

[78] *"The Dawn-Breakers"* p. 98-99.

[79] Ibid p. 100.

[80] Ibid p. 101-102.

and his servant reached the city of Mina, Saudi Arabia where he purchased nineteen lambs. Nine lambs were sacrificed in his name, seven in the name of Quddús, and three in the name of his loyal Ethiopian servant. Not wishing to eat the meat that came from this sacrifice, the Báb distributed it to the poor throughout the neighborhood.[81] Upon reaching the holy city of Mecca, the Báb circumambulated the Kab'ih, often referred to as the Kaaba[82], one of the most sacred sites in Islam. He performed the rites as prescribed.[83]

During his stay in Mecca, the Báb wrote a letter to Mírzá Muhít-i-Kirmání regarding his mission as the Gate to God. The Báb welcomed Muhít's questions about his mission and the letter came to be known as *Sahifiyi-i-Baynu'l-Haramayn*, otherwise known as *The Epistle between the Two Shrines*.[84] Initially, Mírzá Muhít supported the Báb, but his support was not unwavering. The Báb's letter was of little impact and Mírzá Muhít remained hesitant in supporting the Báb's mission.

Continuing through Mecca to Medina, the Báb ran across many who showed concern for him. It was feared that his oppressors would bring him harm or even an early death. In response to these concerns the Báb had this to say:

"I am come into this world to bear witness to the glory of sacrifice. You are aware of the intensity of My longing; you realize the degree of My renunciation. Nay, beseech the Lord

---

[81] *"The Dawn-Breakers"* p. 102-103.

[82] "The name of the temple to which devout Muhammedans make pilgrimage. It is "a square primitive stone building at Mecca, which Muslims believe to have been built by Abraham, and to which the pagan Arabs had from ancient times performed pilgrimages as to their national sanctuary, on which occasion they performed the very same rites and ceremonies now observed by the Muslim pilgrims.'" (*An Encyclopedia of Religions*) p. 207. Original sourced credited to F. A. Klein.

[83] *"The Dawn-Breakers"* p. 103.

[84] Translation provided in a footnote. (*The Dawn-Breakers*) p. 103-104.

your God to hasten the hour of My martyrdom and to accept My sacrifice. Rejoice, for both I and Quddús will be slain on the altar of our devotion to the King of Glory. The blood which we are destined to shed in His path will water and revive the garden of our immortal felicity. The drops of this consecrated blood will be the seed out of which will arise the Mighty Tree of God, the Tree that will gather beneath its all-embracing shadow the people and kindreds of the earth. Grieve not, therefore, if I depart from this land, for I am hastening to fulfill My destiny."[85]

From this we see that Siyyid `Alí Muḥammad Shírází had no fear of death because to him it was martyrdom. He had a mission from God that he was to fulfill. Given his dedication to fulfilling this mission he did not fear martyrdom. To suffer death while declaring his mission was, in his eyes, one step closer to eternal happiness. Rather than worry and fear his imminent death the Báb preferred that his adherents ask God to accept his sacrifice.

After returning to his hometown, the Báb entrusted Quddús to deliver a letter to Ḥájí Mírzá Siyyid 'Alí, the Báb's uncle. Along with this letter was a document titled *Khasá'il-i-Sab'ih*[86] which had detailed the requirements of those who were to follow his Revelation. Ḥájí Mírzá Siyyid 'Alí, although the uncle of Siyyid `Alí Muḥammad Shírází, was unaware of his revelation until having met with Quddús where the letter and document were examined. Because of this meeting with Quddús, Ḥájí Mírzá Siyyid 'Alí would go on to be an ardent supporter, even dying in the name of his nephew.[87] One of

---

[85] "*The Dawn-Breakers*" p. 106.

[86] "The Seven Qualifications" Translation provided in a footnote. (*The Dawn-Breakers*) p. 107.

[87] "As the full significance of the new-born Faith had remained as yet divulged, he was unaware of the full extent of its implications and glory. His conversation with Quddús, however, removed the veil from his eyes. So steadfast became his faith,

the general rules within the *Khasá'il-i-Sab'íh* was that the following statement was to be included in the prayers of his followers; "I bear witness that He whose name is 'Alí-Qabl-i-Muhammad is the servant of the Baqíyyatu'lláh." The Báb is 'Alí-Qabl-i-Muhammad and Bahá'u'lláh is Baqíyyatu'lláh.[88] The recognition of one was not to be without the other.

Upon word of this document getting around, there were those who began to accept its language and speak the words within it. Those in power were dismayed and considered many of those who supported this unknown revolutionary as a blasphemous traitors of Islam. Much of this was likely a result of the declaration relating to those in power where they were, in essence, being asked to step down from their position, which, coming from their perspective, was a reason for concern. The punishment given to Quddús and his newly acquainted adherent of the Báb's faith was discomforting to say the least. They were whipped, chained, and had their beards burned. Having endured these abuses, they were led through the city as an example of what would follow for those who decided to follow this new revolutionary known as the Báb.[89]

As would be the case, this was not the end of trouble for the Báb or Bábís, as word of the Báb was still rampant throughout the area, and he was gaining new adherents at an alarming rate. The governor at this time, Husayn Khan, decided to take matters into his own hands by sending men off to have the Báb arrested. As these men run across the Báb, they describe him as "[A] youth who wore a green sash and a small turban after the manner of the Siyyids who are in the trading profession. He was on horseback, and was

---

(continued from previous page) and so profound grew his love for the Báb, that he consecrated his whole life to His service." "*The Dawn-Breakers*" p. 107.

[88] Ibid p. 107.

[89] For the full account of this incident refer to *The Dawn-Breakers* p. 109.

followed by an Ethiopian servant who was in charge of his belongings."[90]

The Báb recognized these men and rather than flee, he decided to engage them in conversation, acknowledging that he was aware of their objective. His words were, "The governor has sent you to arrest Me. Here am I; do with Me as you please. By coming out to meet you, I have curtailed the length of your march, and have made it easier for you to find Me. [...] I swear by the righteousness of Him who created man, distinguished him from among the rest of His creatures, and caused his heart to be made the seat of His sovereignty and knowledge, that all My life I have uttered no word but the truth and had no other desire except the welfare and advancement of My fellow-men. I have disdained My own ease and have avoided being the cause of pain or sorrow to anyone. I know that you are seeking Me. I prefer to deliver Myself into your hands, rather than subject you and your companions to unnecessary annoyance for My sake."[91]

Many may find the idea of subjecting oneself to such a situation, especially considering his position as a revolutionary, to be an unwise choice, though if this is genuinely how the Báb presented himself, then it is easy to see how he could gather such a following. To speak as such and to introduce himself in that manner prompts his persecutors to question their actions against him, as is the case in this situation. These men who were sent by their governing authority were willing to let the Báb run free to avoid the wrath of Husayn Khan, but the Báb would have none of it. He understood their objective, was appreciative of their concern for his life but allowed them to take him back

---

[90] *"The Dawn-Breakers"* p. 109-110.

[91] Ibid p. 110.

to their governor.

When the Báb faced the governor, he was treated with much disrespect, at one point even being hit with enough force to knock the turban off his head. Given the circumstances, he was asked to make an address in front of the inhabitants of the city stating that he was not the promised Qá'im. Strangely enough, contrary to such figures of the past, he did just this. At this time the Báb stated:

"The condemnation of God be upon him who regards me either as a representative of the Imám or the gate thereof. The condemnation of God be also upon whosoever imputes to me the charge of having denied the unity of God, of having repudiated the prophethood of Muḥammad, the Seal of the Prophets, of having rejected the truth of any of the messengers of old, or of having refused the guardianship of 'Alí, the Commander of the Faithful, or of any of the imáms who have succeeded him."[92]

Whether this move was made by the Báb to protect his loved ones residing within this vicinity or whether he had another prerogative altogether is hard to discern, but given the sequence of events that preceded this encounter with the governor, it is clear that the Báb did not doubt the continuation of his faith. The Báb's dismissal of doubt may also have had to do with the fact that around this time Bahá'u'lláh was on the rise. Shortly after giving his address to the city inhabitants, the Báb celebrated his first full year of having declared his mission.

An interview with the Báb that was meant to prove his claims a falsehood later ensued. This interview, or rather

---

[92] "*The Dawn-Breakers*" p. 110-112.

series of interviews, was with Siyyid Yaḥyáy-i-Darábí[93], a man of high status whose intellect surpassed that of any who spoke with him. With each interview, Siyyid Yaḥyáy-i-Darábí grew more convinced that the claim of the Báb was true and by the end of the third interview he no longer had doubt. How the Báb brought about the interviewer's acceptance was by revealing a commentary on the Súrih of Kawthar/Kauthar.

Before seeing what about this commentary was so impressive, there is a critical question that must first be addressed; What is the Súrih of Kawthar? The answer to this question is answered in the Holy Qur'an where it states:
"This very brief early Makkan Sura sums up in a single meaningful word Kauthar (Abundance) the doctrine of spiritual Riches through devotion and sacrifice. The converse also follows: indulgence in hatred means the cutting off of all hopes of this life and the Hereafter."[94]

Súrih 108 of the Holy-Qur'an, titled *Al-Kauthar* only comprises of three verses which state; "To thee have We granted the Abundance. Therefore to thy Lord turn in Prayer and Sacrifice. For he who hateth thee,- He will be cut off (From Future Hope)."[95]

How can a commentary on a chapter in the Qur'an that numbers a total of three verses be so impressive? The Báb had spent five hours compiling his commentary and when

---

[93] "Concerning him, `Abdu'l-Bahá has written the following: "This remarkable man, this precious soul, had committed to memory no less than thirty thousand traditions, and was highly esteemed and admired by all classes of people. He had achieved universal renown in Persia, and his authority and erudition were widely and fully recognized.'" (*The Dawn-Breakers*) p. 122-123. The source credits a manuscript relating to martyrdoms in Persia.

[94] *"The Holy Qur-an: English translation of the meanings and Commentary"* p. 2018.

[95] Ibid p. 2019.

finished it numbered two thousand verses.[96]

After the two-year mark of the Báb's declaration, he found himself in the hands of 'Abdu'l-Hamid Khan at the request of governor Husayn Khan. As the Báb was being led to the governor, an outbreak of cholera was in full effect which resulted in a scene of much disarray. At this time 'Abdu'l-Hamid Khan brought the Báb with him to check on his family before finishing his objective, at which point he discovered that his son was very ill. Seeing that his options were minimal 'Abdu'l-Hamid Khan begged that the Báb heal his child and that if he did so, he would allow him to run free. In response, "The Báb, who was in the act of performing His ablutions and was preparing to offer the prayer of dawn, directed him to take some of the water with which He was washing his face to his son and requested him to drink it."[97] Sure enough, the boy began showing signs of recovery and Abdu'l-Hamid Khan wrote a letter to the governor asking that he allow the Báb to run free as thanks for saving his child. The governor granted this request with the contingency that he not be allowed to return.

The Báb respected the wishes of the governor and left to find residence in Isfahan, where he was granted stay by the governor of this territory, Manúchihr Khán. Not only was he allowed in, but he was provided a residence with the Imám-Jum'ih, leading religious authority figure of the province. One night the Imám-Jum'ih requested that Siyyid `Alí Muḥammad Shírází reveal a commentary on the Súrih of Va'l-'Asr/Al'Asr, another chapter of the Qur'an that comprises of only three verses. The Báb was delighted. The verses of this chapter read as follows:

---

[96] "*A Thematic Analysis and Summary of The Persian Bayán*" p. 1. To compare, the Qur'an in its entirety numbers about 6,500 verses.
[97] "*The Dawn-Breakers*" p. 136.

"By the time, verily man, is in loss, except such as have Faith, And do righteous deeds, And (join together) In the mutual enjoining of truth, and of patience and constancy."[98]

Within a commentary on this chapter in the Qur'an, it is stated that "[a]n appeal is made to Time as one of the creations of Allah, of which everyone knows something but of which no one can fully explain the exact significance. Time searches out and destroys everything material."[99]
By the end of the night the Báb had completed his commentary which numbered roughly one-third of the Qur'an, or about two thousand verses.[100]

He soon gathered quite the following in Isfahan, and many people came to him seeking answers. In one instance, the Báb was questioned as to the origins of Islam, and through this questioning, he had written fifty pages in a two-hour period detailing his response. But with enormous popularity and praise comes criticism and opposition from others, as many of the ecclesiastical leaders of this province began to feel that if the Báb were to continue to grow his following, their authority and knowledge would be undermined. The problem was that whenever someone was to confront the Báb, the best argument was for the Báb or his followers to request the oppressor to produce a writing of the same caliber, to which nobody felt equipped for the task.[101]

Another instance where the Báb seemingly performed a miracle, such as curing the sick child before arriving in Isfahan, was when he helped grant a couple their wish to have a baby. Despite trying, the couple had been

---

[98] Súrih 103. (*The Holy Qur-an: English translation of the meanings and Commentary*) p. 2003.

[99] Ibid p. 2003.

[100] *"The Dawn-Breakers"* p. 138

[101] Ibid p. 139-140.

unsuccessful in their previous efforts. The account states:

"Mírzá Ibráhím turned to his Guest and said "My brother, Mírzá Muḥammad-'Alí has no child. I beg You to intercede in his behalf and to grant his heart's desire." The Báb took a portion of the food with which He had been served, placed it on His own hands on a platter, and handed it to His host, asking him to take it to Mírzá Muḥammad-'Alí and his wife. "Let them both partake of this," he said; "their wish will be fulfilled." By virtue of that portion which the Báb had chosen to bestow upon her, the wife of Mírzá Muḥammad-'Alí conceived and in due time gave birth to a girl..."[102]

Another of the Báb's miracles occurred while on his way to Tabriz, Iran. Accompanied by guards, the Báb headed toward Tabriz, where he would be imprisoned three years into his mission. The account states:
"In the morning, as we were setting out from Milán, an old woman brought a scald-headed child, whose head was so covered with scabs that it was white down to the neck, and entreated His Holiness to heal him. The guards would have forbidden her but His Holiness prevented them, and called the child to Him. Then He drew a handkerchief over its head and repeated certain words; which he had no sooner done than the child was healed. And in the place about two hundred persons believed and underwent a true and sincere conversion."[103]
Following the Báb's short-term incarceration in the city of Tabriz, he was transferred to the castle of Máh-Kú where he remained in the custody of 'Alí Khán-i-Máh-Kú'í. This castle, pictured in *The Dawn-Breakers*, has been described as "[A] solid, four-towered, stone edifice, [that] occupies the summit

---

[102] *"The Dawn-Breakers"* p. 141.

[103] Footnote (*The Dawn-Breakers*) p. 153. The source is credited to *Tárikh-i-Jadíd*, otherwise known as (*The New History*) *of Mirza Ali-Muhammad the Báb* by Husayn Hamadani, translated by E. G. Browne, 1893, p. 221-222.

of a mountain [and] at the foot of which lies the town Máh-Kú."[104] Máh-Kú is also known as Jabál-i-Basít, or as the Báb called it 'the Open Mountain.'[105] During his imprisonment in the castle of Máh-Kú, the Báb spent much of his time writing the *Persian Bayán*, which contained roughly eight thousand verses.[106]

The *Persian Bayán* translates to 'Persian Exposition,' and by this, it can be understood that the *Persian Bayán* is a comprehensive description of the laws and beliefs found within the Báb's faith. Within the *Persian Bayán*, one can also see that the Báb urges his followers to seek 'Him whom God would make Manifest,' referring to Bahá'u'lláh. Among his other writings during his stay in Máh-Kú, one can find *Dalá'il-i-Sab'ih*, which translates to '*The Book of Seven Proofs*.' As one might have guessed this book was written to address those who question his claim to prophethood and thus request proof.[107] Overall, it could be said that the Báb enjoyed his imprisonment in the castle of Máh-Kú, which may sound absurd, but after having gained the praise of 'Alí Khán-i-Máh-Kú'í, the man whose custody he was placed in, the Báb was treated very well. 'Alí Khán-i-Máh-Kú'í even went on to become an ardent believer in the Báb and allowed him visitors and offered to bring him anything he wished. On one occasion, he even requested that the Báb take his daughter's hand in marriage, but the Báb declined to do so. The Báb's captivity in Máh-Kú lasted nine months, at which time it was now four years since the declaration of his mission.

What brought about the Báb's desire to declare his mission?

---

[104] "*The Dawn-Breakers*" p. 155-156.

[105] Ibid p. 155 & 189.

[106] "*A Thematic Analysis and Summary of The Persian Bayan*" p. 1. To compare, the Qur'an in its entirety numbers about 6,500 verses.

[107] "*The Seven Proofs*" p. 1.

The Báb can answer this himself where he says: "The spirit of prayer which animates My soul is the direct consequence of a dream which I had in the year before the declaration of My Mission. In My vision I saw the head of the Imám Ḥusayn, the Siyyidu'sh-Shuhada', which was hanging upon a tree. Drops of blood dripped profusely from His lacerated throat. With feelings of unsurpassed delight, I approached that tree and, stretching forth My hands, gathered a few drops of that sacred blood, and drank them devoutly. When I awoke, I felt that the Spirit of God had permeated and taken possession of My soul. My heart was thrilled with the joy of His divine presence, and the mysteries of His Revelation were unfolded before My eyes in all their glory."[108]

The significance of this vision can easily be overlooked. In recounting that the promised Mahdi is of Imam Husayn's descendants, then the presence and ingestion of his blood suggests to the Báb that he is undoubtedly the promised one. A vision of this sort could be interpreted as a divine message, which would have provoked the Báb to make his claim.

Following the end of the Báb's imprisonment in the castle of Máh-Kú is his imprisonment in the castle of Chihríq, often referred to as Jabál-i-Shadíd or as the Báb called it, Grievous Mountain.[109] This term of imprisonment was not as luxurious as the one that preceded it. Yaḥyá Khán-i-Kurd, the man placed in charge of the Báb in this case, was given strict orders meant to prevent him from befriending the Báb as the last officer had. This stay at Grievous Mountain was not long though as he was soon transferred to Urúmíyyih where he was given their most difficult horse to ride, sort of just as entertainment, but what followed had many in awe as this horse was perfectly content with the Báb. Many consider this

---

[108] *"The Dawn-Breakers"* p. 163

[109] Ibid p. 155 & 189.

to be one of his many miracles.[110]

From Urúmíyyih the Báb was moved to Tabriz where the Nizámu'l-'Ulama' asked him; "Whom do you claim to be?" to which he responded by saying "I am, I am, the promised One! I am the One whose name you have for a thousand years invoked, at whose mention you have risen, whose advent you have longed to witness, and the hour of whose Revelation you have prayed God to hasten. Verily I say, it is incumbent upon the peoples of both the East and West to obey My word and to pledge allegiance to My person."[111] Having made such a bold statement there was much silence, until at last a response was given by Mullá Muḥammad: "You wretched and immature lad of Shíráz! [...] [Y]ou perverse and contemptible follower of Satan!'"[112]

The argument did not end there, because the Nizámu'l-'Ulama' requested proof of his claim. The Báb declared: "The power to produce such evidence has been given to Me by God. Within the space of two days and two nights, I declare Myself able to reveal verses of such number as will equal the whole of the Qur'án."[113]

From Tabriz, the Báb was transferred back to Chihríq to be under the eye of Yaḥyá Khán-i-Kurd once again. It is here

---

[110] "The inhabitants of Urúmíyyih, who had been informed of the intention of the prince, had filled the public square, eager to witness what might befall the Báb. As soon as the horse was brought to Him He quietly caressed it and placed His foot in the stirrup. The horse stood still and motionless beside Him as if conscious of the power which was dominating it. The multitude that watched this most unusual spectacle marveled at the behavior of the animal. To their simple minds this extraordinary incident appeared little short of a miracle." (*The Dawn-Breakers*) p. 193.

[111] Ibid p. 195-196.

[112] Ibid p. 196.

[113] "*The Dawn-Breakers*" p. 196.

where he undertook the writing of the *Khutbiy-i-Qahríyyih*[114] where he speaks of his mistreatment and the disbelief in his claims that he had recently been presented with.

The death of Siyyid `Alí Muḥammad Shírází occurred on July 9th of 1850, but not before disagreement between the State and the Bábís broke out into violence. A passage from *The Dawn-Breakers* quoting Grand Vazír of Náṣiri'd-Dín Sháh shows the perspective of someone in favor of the Báb's execution. He explains his reasoning in the following words:

"[T]he storm which the Faith of the Siyyid-i-Báb has provoked in the hearts of my fellow-countrymen! Nothing short of his public execution can, to my mind, enable this distracted country to recover its tranquility and peace. Who dare compute the forces that have perished in the course of the engagements at Shaykh Tabarsí? Who can estimate the efforts exerted to secure that victory? No sooner had the mischief that convulsed Mázindarán been suppressed, than the flames of another sedition blazed forth in the province of Fárs, bring in its wake so much suffering to my people. We had no sooner succeeded in quelling the revolt that had ravaged the south, then another insurrection breaks out in the north, sweeping in its vortex Zanján and its surroundings. If you are able to advise a remedy, acquaint me with it, for my sole purpose is to ensure the peace and honor of my countrymen."[115]

The Grand Vazír later commanded that the Báb be executed at the hands of colonel Sám Khán. He was to be shot in the courtyard of the barracks of Tabriz, in the center of the city.

Awaiting his execution, the Báb had a request to ask of the

---

[114] 'Sermon of Wrath'. Translation offered in a footnote of *The Dawn-Breakers* p. 199.

[115] "*The Dawn-Breakers*" p. 299-300.

few Bábís who were present with him. His request was –
"Tomorrow, will be the day of My martyrdom. Would that
one of you might now arise and, with his own hands, end My
life. I prefer to be slain by the hand of a friend rather than by
that of the enemy."[116] Only one had declared that he would
do so, given that he would do anything the Báb wished him
to, but the other Bábís would not allow it.

In preparation for the Báb's execution, he was suspended
from a rope alongside a youth who insisted on being
executed alongside his Master. Two-hundred and fifty men
lined up with guns and fired.

"As soon as the cloud of smoke had cleared away, an
astounded multitude were looking upon a scene which their
eyes could scarcely believe. There, standing before them alive
and unhurt, was the companion of the Báb, whilst He
Himself had vanished uninjured from their sight. Though the
cords with which they were suspended had been rent in
pieces by the bullets, yet their bodies had miraculously
escaped the volley."[117]

The Báb appeared to be unfazed by what had occurred and
merely wished to finish the conversation he was having prior
to having been interrupted for his execution. Having
concluded his discussion, he allowed himself to be suspended
once more and at this time an end was brought to the life of
Siyyid `Alí Muḥammad Shírází. He was thirty-one years old.

Among the many writings of the Báb that have not been
introduced in the above text, there are the *Kitáb-i-Panj-Sha'n*
or the 'Five Modes'[118] where he speaks on how the sixth

---

[116] Ibid p. 302.

[117] Ibid p. 305.

[118] *"Kitáb-i-Panj-Sha'n"* p. 1.

Naw-Rúz[119] of his mission shall be the last one he will be able to celebrate on earth, alluding to his imminent death. There is also the *Kitáb-i-Asmá'* or 'The Book of Names' where the Báb goes on to say "O ye who are invested with the Bayán! Be ye watchful on the Day of Resurrection, for on that Day ye will firmly believe in the Váḥid of the Bayán, though this, even as your past religion which proved of no avail, can in no wise benefit you, unless ye embrace the Cause of Him Whom God shall make manifest and believe in that which He ordaineth. Therefore take ye good heed lest ye shut yourselves out from Him Whom is the Fountain-head of all Messengers and Scriptures, while ye hold fast to parts of the teaching which have emanated from these sources."[120] Here the Báb is speaking to the Bábís saying that Bahá'u'lláh will follow the death of himself and that the mission does not end here but instead continues through Bahá'u'lláh. Ultimately, he wanted the Bábís to remain steadfast in their faith but accept 'Him Whom God shall make manifest' as his successor.

---

[119] "[T]he Bahá'í and Iranian new year, which occurs on the date of the vernal equinox, about 21 March. It is one of the nine Bahá'í holy days on which work is suspended." (*Naw-Rúz: The Bahá'í New Year*) p. 1.

[120] "*Selections from the Writings of the Báb*" p. 62-63. The source is credited to " *Kitáb-i-Asmá*'" Ch. 17.

## Muhammad Ahmad (A. D. 1844 – 1885)

In the North African country of Sudan there was a Mahdi claimant who went by the name Muhammad Ahmad ibn Abdullah[121], and although details of his youth are hard to come by, some accounts state that he had, by the age of twelve, memorized the Qur'an by heart. Because of this and other feats of similar intrigue, Muhammad Ahmad was not required to work for a living. His brothers took it upon themselves to see that his needs were met.[122]

On this note, his story begins with his residence in Aba Island, Sudan. By this time, he and his brothers were capable of making a living for themselves and were gifted with a luxurious hut, though this is not where Muhammad Ahmad wished to reside. Rather than stay in a lavish hut, Muhammad Ahmad preferred a cave-like hole in the ground. He had no reason to labor, given that his brothers would care for him, but he still chose to work the fields now and then. He was very devout with his search for God and "sometimes weeks would pass before he emerged into the light of day out of the dark hole in which he was praying and singing and fasting."[123] According to the writings of James Darmesteter (d. 1894) there are only two truly authentic accounts of Muhammad Ahmad's story.

"One is the letter of a Frenchman born in Soudan, who saw him at Khartoum – M. Mousa Peney, son of Dr. Peney, one of the bravest of explorers in the Soudan, the first European

---

[121] Also spelled Muhammad Ahmad bin Abd Allah. (*The Mahdi of Allah*) p. 47.

[122] "Moreover, from his childhood, Mohammed showed that he had a decided vocation; at twelve years old he knew the Koran by heart. When his father died, his two elder brothers, who were boat-builders on the White Nile, seeing that he had talent, supplied his wants, and provided him with means to study under two professors of repute in the neighborhood of Khartoum, Abdel Dagim, and El Gourachi." (*The Mahdi: Past and Present*) Ch. VIII, p. 65-66.

[123] "*The Mahdi of Allah*" p. 50.

who had ever visited Gondokoro. [...] The other, which dives into the very souls of the heroes of the drama, is the report of a consultation of the Ulemas of El Azhar Mosque at Cairo, of which M. Clermont Ganneau, the well-known Orientalist, has kindly communicated his own translation to the author [James Darmesteter]."[124]

From these accounts it can be gathered that Muhammad Ahmad was born in the city of Dongola, Sudan and in the year 1869, at the age of twenty-five, had made his way to Aba Island where his story begins to take shape.

His time spent here can almost be described as a fifteen-year retirement. The behavior Muhammad Ahmad exhibited, such as choosing to reside in a cave-like depression in the ground where he would sit in prayer for days at a time soon made him a curious sight. One tribe, described as 'The neighboring tribe of Beggaras [Beggars?], the most powerful in this region of the Nile"[125] began to regard him as a saint. This would come to form the foundation of his support when he made his claim to Mahdiship in the years to come. Women came to him with prayers that they may have children and men came to him with the hopes of protecting themselves and those they loved from harm.[126] But why would these people come to regard Muhammad Ahmad as the promised Mahdi? The answer is simple; many were not happy with the state of the government, so any who showed opposition in favor of the people over the government, who had a vision for a brighter future was welcomed with open arms.[127]

---

[124] *"The Mahdi: Past and Present"* Ch. VIII, p. 60.

[125] Ibid, Ch. VIII, p. 68. Brackets mine.

[126] "With a credulity that is only paralleled by their ignorance, women besought his prayers that they might have children, men trusted to his incantations to ward off from them the bullets of their foes." (*Osman Digna*) p. 11.

[127] "It is not difficult to imagine with what ease the pious recluse of Aba Island collected a large and appreciative body of supporters. The harassed native of the Sudan was prepared to follow any leader who held before his eyes the vision of brighter days to come and a release from the enormities of the venal Government

Beginning around the end of his fifteen-year retirement, in 1881, Muhammad Ahmad made his claim, that he was the expected Mahdi. He had gone about doing so by sending missionaries to inform others that "[T]he Turkish dominion was about to end, that the Soudan was to rise on every side."[128] Political authorities showed little interest in Ahmad's statements. They felt it was clear he was a false prophet and that others would see through his façade, at which time his limelight would soon fade. Contrary to what political authorities thought, support for Muhammad Ahmad only continued to grow. By the time they decided to act, it was too late. Raouf Pacha, Governor-General, decided to send two hundred men out to Aba Island, from Khartoum, in an attempt to capture Ahmad.[129] Raouf Pacha's dislike for the Sudan Mahdi was likely because the Ulemas of Constantinople and Cairo regarded Ahmad as a false prophet. The Grand Sherif of Mecca, highest priest of Islam, was also of this opinion.[130] To be fair, before having sent these men to capture Muhammad Ahmad, Raouf Pacha had sent a single person requesting that he come to Khartoum of his own volition, to which Muhammad Ahmad replied, "What! By the grace of God and His Prophet. I am the master of this country and never shall I go to Khartoum to justify myself."[131]

The two hundred men thus undertook their journey to the hut of Muhammad Ahmad through unfavorable weather conditions. Upon reaching the shelter they were faced with the sight of dervishes, otherwise known as Muslims who have taken vows of poverty, who were surrounding the hut

---

(continued from previous page) that oppressed him." (*Osman Digna*) p. 12.

[128] *"The Mahdi: Past and Present"* Ch. VIII, p. 69.

[129] Ibid Ch. VIII, p. 69.

[130] *"The Conflict of East and West in Egypt"* p. 142-143.

[131] *"Osman Digna"* p. 14.

while dancing and "repeating the sacred name of Allah."[132] For reasons unknown, the adjutant-major of these two hundred men fired into the crowd, killing one of the dervishes.[133] As a result, the remaining dervishes, likely in an act to defend Muhammad Ahmad, decided it best to fight back.

There were more devout defenders of Muhammad Ahmad hidden within the forest surrounding the area and with this help nearly all the two-hundred men sent to Muhammad Ahmad's hut were killed. Following this incident, Muhammad Ahmad, along with the dervishes and his two brothers, headed off towards Jabal Gedir, otherwise known as "the mountain foretold by the seers of old."[134] Those who recognized the Mahdiship of Muhammad Ahmad were pleased with this course of action, given that many of them expected the second Messiah to show himself in that region.[135] Giegler Pacha then gathered a band of men, numbering seven thousand, before continuing towards Jabal Gedir in an attempt to bring down Muhammad Ahmad. To his surprise, his seven thousand men were met with fifty thousand men who chose to revolt in favor of Muhammad Ahmad. These fifty thousand men were led by the Mahdi claimant's elder brothers, Mohammad and Hamed. In the act

---

[132] *"The Mahdi: Past and Present"* Ch. VIII, p. 69-70.

[133] There are multiple accounts of what occurred here, with this being one of them. Two more accounts can be seen in *Osman Digna* where it states; "According to one, Rauf Pasha sent two young officers with the expedition and promised promotion to the one who took the Mahdi prisoner. Abu el Saud was in command, and anchored in midstream while the two half-company commanders, with visions of glory and promotion floating before them, landed at either end of the island. They were ambuscaded, fired impartially on friend or foe, and, as the steamer refused to draw near the island in order to pick up the stragglers, they were destroyed almost to a man. Another version says that one of the soldiers mistaking a native for the Mahdi shot him; and the villagers then attacked the unready force." p. 14.

[134] *"Osman Digna"* p. 14.

[135] This second Messiah is referring to the descent of Isa that is commonly believed to occur when the Mahdi comes out of hiding.

of defending the promised Mahdi, both brothers met their demise but not without helping reduce the opposing force of seven thousand men to a mere one hundred and fifty.[136]

Given that the seven thousand men were outnumbered by about seven to one, the idea of having one-hundred and fifty survivors, regardless of whether they fled the battlefield or not, may, to some, seem doubtful. It is possible that fifty thousand was an exaggeration, but without getting caught up on the numbers, it still goes to show that they were outnumbered and caught by surprise at the fact that Muhammad Ahmad had such an established defense. Following this incident on Mount Gedir, Muhammad Ahmad went on to overtake Al-Ubayyid, which was later made his capital. The writings of James Darmesteter suggest that Al-Ubayyid fell into his hands in the year 1883.[137] There does appear to be a variance of sorts regarding this account though, as can be seen in the writings of H. C. Jackson, published in 1926, where it is suggested that Mohammed, brother of the proclaimed Mahdi, had died during the overtaking of Al-Ubayyid, rather than during the incident at Mount Gedir. Evidence of this can be seen in the following statement:

"The Mahdi then determined to attack, and arrived before the walls of El Obeid with a large force of Dervishes. By daily prayers and exhortations, he laid before his fanatical adherents the beatific visions of the world to come and all the way of God.' On the morning of September 4th, the first attack was delivered and beaten off with appalling losses to the Mahdiists, among the killed being the Mahdi's brother

---

[136] "*The Mahdi: Past and Present*" Ch. VIII, p. 70-71.

[137] "The temporary governor, the Bavarian Giegler Pacha, concentrated the garrisons of Sennaar, Fachoda, and Kordofan, with the view of leading them against the Mahdi, not for a moment imagining that the provinces which he left ungarrisoned by this step would immediately revolt." (Ibid) Ch. VIII, p. 71.

Mohammad, as well as Yusef, the brother of the Khalifa Abdullahi."[138] This same account goes on to state how due to the actions of the Turkish commander of this time, who appeared to be lacking in initiative, the proclaimed Mahdi and his forces were able to regroup, which ultimately led to the successful overtaking of Al-Ubayyid.

It became clear that the force of Muhammad Ahmad was a formidable one and many attempted to bring him to a halt. Unfortunately, he was already an established threat, as the writings of H. C. Jackson attest. Muhammad Ahmad commanded a force of men with about 21,000 rifles and 19 guns.[139]

Colonel Hicks, a retired English officer, was then placed in command of an expedition put in place by the Egyptian government in the hopes of bringing Muhammad Ahmad's antics to an end. Those placed under the command of Colonel Hicks included eight English officers, 6,000 infantry, 1,000 regulars, 500 cavalries, and a small force of artillery.[140] As it would happen, he and his men were compromised before meeting the forces of Muhammad Ahmad, because while in route for Al-Ubayyid they encountered rebel forces. Colonel Hicks and his men were the victors of this encounter, but as a result, were in need of reinforcements who were unable to reach them.

When meeting Muhammad Ahmad and his men in early November, Colonel Hicks Pasha and his men were

---

[138] "*Osman Digna*" p. 17.

[139] "In a little over two years this rabble had developed into a formidable army that with spears and sticks had succeeded in capturing nearly 21,000 rifles and 19 guns." (*Osman Digna*) p. 18. A chart detailing when, where, and how these guns were accumulated is also provided.

[140] This is also supported in the chronological order of events present in H. C. Jackson's book titled *Osman Digna*.

ambushed. One account states that they held out for three days-time, but in the end, nearly every one of the 11,000 men was killed.[141] It would be almost three weeks before the inhabitants of Khartoum and Cairo would hear of this defeat, to which many province governors switched allegiances, choosing to now side with Muhammad Ahmad, seeing this recent victory as a testament to his Mahdiship.[142] At this news there began much talk of evacuating the area, to which Baker Pasha was placed in command to lead the evacuation. After hearing of Colonel Hicks Pasha's defeat with an 11,000-man force, the 4,000 men now available to them did not seem a proper defense if Muhammad Ahmad chose to head in their direction.

In 1884 General Gordan arrived on the scene. He was also placed in position to watch over the evacuation process. The contents of a letter, shown below, will shed some light on General Gordon's involvement. The letter was addressed to him on January 18th of 1884 by Lord Granville (d. 1891) of London.

"Sir: - Her Majesty's Government are desirous that you should proceed at once to Egypt, to report to them on the military situation in the Sudan and on the measures which it may be advisable to take for the security of the Egyptian garrisons still holding possession in that country, and for the safety of the European population in [Khartoum]. You are also desired to consider and report upon the best mode of effecting the evacuation of the interior of the Sudan, and upon the manner in which the safety and the good administration by the Egyptian government of the ports on

---

[141] "They fought for three days with the courage and hopelessness of that smaller band under Leonidas at Thermopylae; then overcome with heat, thirst, and fatigue, their ammunition gone, they fell where they had, before the fury of the Mahdi's hordes." (*The Conflict of East and West in Egypt*) p. 145-146.

[142] Ibid p. 145.

the seacoast can best be secured. In connection with this subject, you should pay especial consideration to the question of the steps that may usefully be taken to counteract the stimulus which it is feared may possibly be given to the slave trade by the present insurrectionary movement and by the withdrawal of the Egyptian authority from the interior. You will be under the instructions of her Majesty's agent and Consul-General at Cairo, through whom your reports to her Majesty's Government should be sent under flying seal. You will consider yourself authorized and instructed to perform such other duties as the Egyptian Government may desire to entrust to you, and as may be communicated to you by Sir E. Baring. You will be accompanied by Colonel Stewart, who will assist you in the duties thus confided to you. On your arrival in Egypt you will at once communicate with Sir E. Baring, who will arrange to meet you, and will settle with you whether you should proceed directly to Suakin, or should go yourself or dispatch Colonel Stewart to [Khartoum], via the Nile."

A letter addressed to Major Charles George Gordon from Sir Evelyn Baring also gives some insight into the workings of this evacuation of Sudan. "You will bear in mind that the main end to be pursued is the evacuation of the Sudan. This policy was adopted, after a very full discussion, by the Egyptian Government, on the advice of her Majesty's Government. It meets with the full approval his Highness the Khedive, and of the present Egyptian Ministry." A credit of 100,000 pounds was also given to C. G. Gordon.[143] Nowadays that 100,000 pounds would be worth about ten million pounds or twelve million U.S. dollars.

While the details of the evacuation were underway, Valentine Baker suffered a loss of 2,000 men at the hands of Osman Digna (d. 1926), military commander and devout believer in

---

[143] *"The Conflict of East and West in Egypt"* p. 151-152.

the Mahdi claim of Muhammad Ahmad. The clash between these two occurred in early February near Tokar, Sudan. Osman Digna, a merchant of little recognition, was sort of a hot head in his youth.[144] Although Baker Pasha had numbers, outnumbering those of Osman Digna four to one, many of his men had never fired a gun before. One account states: "The Arab force numbered no more than 1,200 and in all probability did not exceed 1,000, yet they routed a force between three and four times its size, killed 96 officers and 2,250 men, besides capturing 4 Krupp guns, 2 Gatlings, 3,000 Remington rifles and carbines, and half a million cartridges and all at an insignificant cost; 16 officers were also wounded."[145]

Ahmad's lieutenant, Osman Digna, then went on to overtake Trinkitat, Sudan.[146] Digna was later confronted in Tokar, Sudan, where he had his recent victory over Valentine Baker. This time the confrontation was with General Graham. The victor of this bout was General Graham. "On the last day of February, Graham marched forth and met and overcame the intrepid lieutenant of the Mahdi on the field where Baker's force had been defeated. This success was followed up by further advances, and on March 13 a decisive victory was won."[147] For the first time there was a chink in the armor of Muhammad Ahmad, but due to higher orders General Graham and his men were forced to leave the scene before chasing down those who were on the run. With the absence of General Graham, Digna was able to gather his remaining, yet scattered, troops.

---

[144] "He was a merchant who had no particular standing in the country, either through birth or piety. He was known to have been somewhat wild in his youth, he had the reputation of being rather a firebrand, and he was not a man who had many friends." (*Osman Digna*) p. 26.

[145] Ibid p. 64.

[146] "*The Conflict of East and West in Egypt*" p. 156-159.

[147] Ibid p. 162.

In a letter to Muhammad Ahmad, Osman Digna detailed an account of his battle wounds and body counts from his encounter in Sinkat.

"I was wounded in the hand, head, and side, but my men carried me outside the fort, and then we all withdrew. We had great difficulty in entering the fort, for there were many Turks at the gates and many of our men were killed. My brother, Feki Mohammad Digna, led the attack with a heart of flint, forcing the entrance and killing many of the Turks with his own sword. One Turk tried to strike him down with his rifle, but he cut the rifle in two with his sword and killed the Turk, but was afterwards killed himself. […] Our losses were 60 men, while the Turks lost 57."[148]

General Gordon, a man whose presence rejoiced the inhabitants of Khartoum, arrived on February 18th with the objective of securing their evacuation. Upon his arrival, General Gordon says; "I come without soldiers, but with God on my side, to redress the evils of this land. I will not fight with any weapons but justice."[149] He gained the support of Khartoum's inhabitants by burning books of the government, destroying instruments of torture, releasing the wrongfully imprisoned, and helping the sick. Much of his role in this ordeal with Muhammad Ahmad is detailed throughout his letters, one of which describes his frustration with his governing bodies. He was sent to Khartoum with the objective of assessing the situation and defining what action should be taken to secure the safety of its inhabitants, yet his advice was never really used. Evidence of this is shown in a letter addressed to Sir Evelyn Baring that states;

"As far as I can understand, the situation is this: You state

---

[148] "Osman Digna" p. 33.

[149] "The Conflict of East and West in Egypt" p. 164-165.

your intentions of not sending any relief up here or to Berber, and you refuse me Zubair. I consider myself free to act according to circumstances. I shall hold on here as long as I can; and if I can suppress the rebellion, I shall do so. If I cannot, I shall retire to the Equator; and leave you the indelible disgrace of abandoning the garrisons of Sennar, Kassala, Berber, and Dongola, with the certainty that you will, eventually, be forced to smash up the Mahdi under great difficulties, if you would retain peace in Egypt."[150]

Much of General Gordon's struggles can be glimpsed in his many letters. Throughout his letters he speaks of evacuation tactics, garrison requests, and even his conversations with Muhammad Ahmad.

On July 31st of 1884 General Gordon was unable to abandon his post in Khartoum. He explains his situation in a letter that states:

"Reading over your telegram of the 5th May, 1884, you ask me to state cause and intention in staying at Khartoum, knowing Government means to abandon Sudan, and in answer I say, I stay at Khartoum because Arabs have shut us up, and will not let us out."[151]

General Gordon's stance on how the battle against Muhammad Ahmad had been progressing is laid out in one of his letters as well. "Take the Tokar business: had Baker been supported, say, by 500 men, he would not have been defeated; yet, after he was defeated, you go and send a force to relieve the town. Had Baker been supported by these 500 men, he would, in all probabilities, been victorious, and would have pushed on to Berber; one and there, Berber

---

[150] This letter has not been dated. (*The Conflict of East and West in Egypt*) p. 169-170.

[151] "*The Conflict of East and West in Egypt*" p. 180.

would not have fallen. What was right to do in February. We sent an expedition in March, so we ought to have sent it in February; and then the worst of it was that, Baker having been defeated, when you did send your expedition to Tokar, Baker's force no longer existed, and his guns resist me at Berber. It is truly deplorable, the waste of men and money, on account of our indecision."[152]

General Gordon's frustration grows because he has continued to ask for reinforcements but has received no word that his need will be granted. He saw that the men before him failed for this same reason, their request for help not having been granted until it was too late. General Gordan found himself in the same situation as those who came before him, given that Lord Wolseley, another man tasked with securing an evacuation who arrived in Egypt on September 8th, was unable to assist him when needed. Lord Wolseley was given the objective of rescuing General Gordon and Colonel Stewart, General Gordon's lieutenant.[153] November 14th arrived, and Lord Wolseley had yet to reach Khartoum to rescue General Gordon but had received a letter from him dated November 4th stating that although he was still alive, he had not escaped danger, as Muhammad Ahmad was only about eight hours away, and heading in his direction. Even if he were able to hold out, there were just enough provisions to get him through one month. Meanwhile, General Stewart was repelling a force of 10,000 rebels with a meager 1,500 men.[154]

---

[152] "*Conflict of East and West in Egypt*" p. 181-182.

[153] "In the government's letter of instructions, dated October 8, he was informed that the primary object of his expedition was the rescue of General Gordon and Colonel Stewart." (Ibid) p. 181.

[154] "On the 8th of January, General Stewart, with a picked force of about 1,500 men, was dispatched from Korti straight across the desert to Metemneh, there to meet the steamers that General Gordon had sent out from Khartoum. [...] All went well with General Stewart's desert journey, till he neared the wells of Abu Klea, less than twenty-five miles from Metemneh. He encamped near them on the 16th of

Come the 14th of December, Lord Wolseley had still not reached General Gordon, who at the time had this to say:
"Our troops in Khartoum are suffering from lack of provisions...We want you to come quickly."[155]

General Gordon would not make it out alive, as Khartoum ended up falling into the hands of Muhammad Ahmad on January 26th, 1885. How General Gordon met his fate is uncertain, but he was likely killed fighting off the force of Muhammad Ahmad. Fortunately, his last request was granted, as he had said:
"If Khartoum falls, then go quietly back to Cairo, for you will only lose men and spend money uselessly in carrying out the campaign."[156] The troops did not go all the way back to Cairo but did fall back to the Egyptian border.

Dating back to September[157] of 1844, a letter written by Muhammad Ahmad, addressed to Major Charles George Gordon stated:
"I am the one who invites to God, and the Khalifa of the Apostle of God (God bless him and give him peace) and that I am the Mahdi, the expected one, and this is no boast."[158]

---

(continued from previous page) January, and on the 17th his force was attacked by 10,000 rebels. His troops fought as Englishmen always fight; and the rebels, with all their superiority of numbers, were repulsed. The English loss was sixty-five killed and nearly a hundred wounded." (Ibid) p. 187.

[155] *"Conflict of East and West in Egypt"* p. 188.

[156] Ibid p. 194.

[157] "The letter is not dated in the manuscript. From the sources available it appears that Gordon received only three formal letters from the Mahdi. [...] Of these three the first one, which was received by Gordon March 22, 1884, is translated in full in Major (now Sirdar) Wingate's book: *Mahdiism and the Egyptian Sudan* (1891) pp. 111-115 and is dated March 10, 1844. The second letter was received by Gen. Gordon Sept. 9, 1884. [...] The third letter was received by Gordon Oct. 22, 1884. [...] This points at once to our letter as the one Gordon received Sept. 9 [...], but as there is a possibility of other letters of which no mention has been found, further proof is necessary." (*A Letter from the Mahdi Muhammad Ahmad*) p. 382-383.

[158] *"A Letter from the Mahdi Muhammad Ahmad"* p. 378.

In this same letter he states many reasons as to why C. G. Gordon, should accept the ways of God and describes what punishments await if he and his men decide to do otherwise. "[If], on our arrival, we find you Muslim then all will be well; but if not 'then God will accomplish what is decreed'. 'And they who do wrong shall know with what treatment they shall be treated in the hereafter.'"[159]

Here Muhammad Ahmad is referring to the Qur'an, specifically Súrih 8 titled *Al-Anfal* where, in section 6, verses 45-46, it states:

"O ye who believe! When ye meet a force, be firm, and call Allah in remembrance much (and often); That ye may prosper: And obey Allah and His Messenger; and fall into no disputes, lest ye lose heart and your power depart; And be patient and persevering: For Allah is with those who patiently persevere."[160]

Many of Muhammad Ahmad's other letters can be found in the writings of General Sir Francis Reginald Wingate (d. 1953). "There are in this letter-book one hundred thirty-three letters, ninety nine of which are from the Mahdi."[161]

It should go without question that Muhammad Ahmad differed from the Mahdi claimants that came before him, given that he primarily led militarily rather than spiritually. What ultimately brought about the end of Osman Digna and Muhammad Ahmad? Well oddly enough, although Muhammad Ahmad's time was extensively spent in battle, he did not meet his demise on the battlefield. He died along the White Nile between Khartoum and Omdurman on June 22nd,

---

[159] Ibid p. 381.

[160] *"The Holy Qur-an: English translation of the meaning and Commentary"* p. 483.

[161] Ibid p. 387. Reference to the book mentioned in the previous footnote, *Mahdiism and the Egyptian Sudan.*

1885 of either food poisoning or typhoid fever.[162] A vaccine for this fever was not available until the mid-1890s through the help of Almroth Wright.

Muhammad Ahmad's place of burial is Omdurman, Sudan. His tomb has suffered damage throughout the years but it has also been restored. As for Osman Digna, he was captured, and when caught had this to say:
"I do not run away, but now, as ever, and in accordance with my master's commands, I turn my face away from the unbelievers."[163]

Those who captured Osman Digna had never seen him in person, but given Digna's reputation, were able to identify him by his battle wounds. "Look and see if there is a sword wound in the middle of the head and a bullet wound upon the left wrist, and see if there is a mark of a bayonet in his back. If you find them then you will know that this is he whom we want."[164] His capture occurred in January of 1900 and on the 21st of January he was placed in the prison of Rosetta in Egypt. When questioned by General Wingate, Osman Digna stated:
"I am a soldier, as you are, and it is my duty to obey orders. Before the battle my master, the Khalifa, placed the women of his harem in my charge. It was my duty to look after them. By the time I had assured their safety the battle was over. I could do nothing and fled. I had hoped to escape across the sea to Arabia, and should have succeeded but for the treachery of the Gemilab sheikh."[165]

---

[162] "Whether Mohammad Ahmed died of typhoid or poison – as was suggested – his sudden demise did not lead to the trouble and unrest that might have been expected to ensue on the passing away of so notable a personage." (*Osman Digna*) p. 109.

[163] "*Osman Digna*" p. 165.

[164] Ibid p. 165.

[165] "*Osman Digna*" p. 165-166.

Osman Digna was later transferred to Tora, Egypt which was then followed by a transfer to Wadi Halfa, Sudan. His imprisonment here was rather luxurious, but after requesting that his wives be able to join him, was surprised to find that his wives declined to do so. He was not a good husband. His son, in the year 1917, had wished to visit him, but Osman Digna paid him no mind. In the year 1924, at the age of 90, Osman Digna was granted the opportunity to perform Hajj, and while returning from Mecca resided in a home just outside of Wadi Halfa until his demise, but not without being under the watchful eye of guards.[166]

---

[166] Ibid p. 169.

## Mirza Ghulam Ahmad (A. D. 1835 – 1908)

In recounting the details of Mirza Ghulam Ahmad's claim to Mahdiship it is important to note that not only did he claim to be the promised Messiah of the Muhammadan world, but also claimed to be the promised Messiah for both the Christians and Hindus. In his 1904 lecture titled *The Future of Islam*, he states that his claims are not of his own accord but rather that of the Mighty God of earth and heavens. He also claims that God revealed to him that Jesus died an ordinary death, but more on this later.

Mirza Ghulam Ahmad's interest in religion started when he began studying the Qur'an as a youth in Qadian, India. He was tutored at home since there were not many public schooling programs in Qadian, and most of the education he received revolved around the Qur'an. Alongside his studies of the Qur'an, he was taught Urdu, a language he later used in his writings. In addition, Mirza Ghulam Ahmad was taught medicine thanks to his father Mirza Ghulam Murtaza (d. 1876), and since there were no doctors in the area he often looked over those in his district free of charge.[167]

One testament to his faith and belief in the Qur'an can be seen where his father, when speaking of his son, asserts that if one hopes to find his son they must check the mosque because he spends much of his time there, taking little interest in worldly affairs.[168] When he wasn't at the mosque he was likely pacing side to side in his bedroom while either reading or writing.[169] Since he preferred to pace the width of his room he chose to keep an inkpot at either end so that he never chanced running out of ink while in the midst of

---

[167] *"The Promised Messiah"* p. 13.

[168] *"Mirza Ghulam Ahmad of Qadian"* p. 17-18.

[169] This habit of pacing around the room while reading or writing followed him throughout his life. (*Mirza Ghulam Ahmad of Qadian*) p. 20.

writing. Some of the books he is known to have studied outside of the Qur'an at this time, from the ages of 13 to 20, include *Dala'il al-Khayrat* (Waymarks of Benefits and the Brilliant Burst of Lights in the Remembrance of Blessings on the Chosen Prophet), *Masnavi* (Spiritual Couplets), *Tazkirat al-Awliya* (Biographies of the Saints), and *Futuhul Ghaib* (Revelations of the Unseen). The *Ṣaḥīḥ al-Bukhārī*, one part of a hadith collection, was also a favorite of his.

This was by no means the entirety of his studies because by the age of 16, he had thoroughly studied both the Bible and the Vedas, annotating them with just as much care as he had the Qur'an. Through these studies, Mirza Ghulam Ahmad said that he had found nearly 3,000 objections raised against the Holy Prophet Muhammad.[170] He was very thorough with his studies, as can be seen by the account of a cart driver that had driven him 11 miles in 2 hours. In this instance, Ahmad chose to read *Al- Fātiḥa,* the first Súrih in the Qur'an, for the duration of his ride. It contains only seven verses.[171]

Mirza Mubarak Ahmad, grandson of Mirza Ghulam Ahmad offers insight into his grandfather's devotion where he quotes a passage from Mirza Ghulam's *Chashma-i-Masihi (Fountain of Christianity)*;
"O Thou, to Whom my soul, my heart and every particle of mine are dedicated, open wide to me, out of Thy Mercy and Grace, all the gates of Divine [Realization]. The philosopher who seeks to know Thee through his intellect and reasoning, is devoid of intellect and reasoning, for the secret way that leads to Thee is far above reasoning and intellect. None of these has gained any awareness of Thy sacred Precincts,

---

[170] Not only had he studied the Bible but also the commentaries of some Christian writers. (Ibid) p. 20.

[171] *Al- Fātiḥa*, the seven-verse chapter, speaks of 'the perfect prayer' and is itself a prayer. For the account of the cart driver, refer to *Mirza Ghulam Ahmad of Qadian*, p. 21.

whoever has gained such awareness has gained it through Thy Boundless Grace."[172]

With statements such as this it is easy to see how people would grow interested in what he had to say. After all, he was stating that what he sought after could not be attained through intellect, but only through Divine Will. He was suggesting that the philosophers have gone about it the wrong way, and then suggests an alternative. People began to wonder if maybe he was right.

Another account of the previous quote, this time written in verse, can be seen below:

"O You, for Whom I would sacrifice my life,
My heart, and every particle of my being!
With Your mercy, open for me
All the paths to recognizing You.

The Philosopher who seeks You
Through reason, is insane;
The hidden path that leads to You
Lies far from reason's domain.

None of them ever found
Your Holy Abode
Only through Your limitless Grace
Has anyone ever found the Road.

You give both the worlds
To the lovers of Your Countenance;
But the two worlds are nothing
In the eyes of Your servants.

With just one look
Stop all this war and confrontation;

---

[172] *"The Promised Messiah"* p. 14.

72

The world truly needs
A sign of Your manifestation.

Show a sign
So that the world may be filled with Your Light;
And every denier of the Faith
May sing Your praises day and night.

I would not be the least troubled
If the whole world was to turn upside down;
I am only worried lest Your Luminous Path
Should become lost and unknown.

Nothing comes out of religious debates
Put an end to them with Your Mighty signs.

Stir people's consciences with earthquakes
So that fear may bring them to Your Gates.

In the garb of an earthquake
Make a fountain of mercy flow;
How long will Your wailing servant
Languish in his sorrow?"[173]

Mirza Ghulam Ahmad maintained that because he was so devout and obedient to the Holy Prophet Muhammad, God had bestowed upon him the position of being the messiah of not only Islam, Christianity, and Hinduism, but all principle religions, including Buddhism and Sikhism. In one instance he refers to himself as the 'Champion of God in the mantels of all the prophets.'[174] Mirza Ghulam also wanted to make it clear that where he differed from Muhammad was that rather than being a law-giving prophet he was the prophet to unite

---

[173] *"Chashma-e-Masihi (Fountain of Christianity)"* p. 71-72.

[174] *"Mirza Ghulam Ahmad of Qadian"* p. 8-9.

all religions under Islam, which led many to write him off as Satan himself.[175]

In the early 1850s, Mirza Ghulam Ahmad had an arranged marriage to his cousin Hurmat Babi. They went on to have two sons, Sultan Ahmad and Fazal Ahmad, who were both born in the first four years of the marriage.[176] Although this marriage did later fall apart, he did remarry and have more children.

Come 1864, Mirza Ghulam Ahmad began work as a clerk in the civil administration of the Sialkot district. Four years later, he resigned due to a family emergency. His mother, Chiragh Bibi, had grown ill. She was a generous woman to those in poverty. Now home, he continued his endless study of religious doctrines such as the Torah and commentaries on eastern religions. To avoid being bothered while studying, he arranged to have his food placed in a basket so he could pull it up to his study/bedroom whenever he desired food, which wasn't all that often.

His father grew irritated with his ways and was upset when he found out that his son had turned down an opportunity to work in the city of Kapurthala. All Mirza Ghulam Ahmad had to say in response to his father's objections was;
"I have no desire to take up any kind of service. All I ask for is two suits of course homespun cloth and a little bread of whatever kind and quality might be available. That is all."[177]
Mirza Ghulam Murtaza was proud of his son's devotion, he only wished he would allow himself to have more in life than devotion and study, whereas Mirza Ghulam Ahmad saw no reason to spend his time elsewhere.

---

[175] *"Mirza Ghulam Ahmad of Qadian"* p. 8-9.

[176] Ibid p. 19.

[177] Ibid p. 35.

In the year 1875, Mirza Ghulam Ahmad, taking the advice given him in a vision, decided to start fasting. He did this in secrecy by simply feeding his food to the poor from his window to avoid alarming his father. He would only eat a single meal after sunset. Over a period of 2-3 weeks, he gradually reduced his food intake. By the end of it all, he was supposedly only consuming a few ounces of bread every twenty-four hours for the next 8-9 months. It is during this time that he experienced what he described as 'spiritual mysteries' where he met saints and prophets of the past in a state of complete wakefulness. Mirza Ghulam Ahmad also claims to have seen colorful 'columns of spiritual light' that brought him feelings of ecstasy that have no comparison.[178] Many will attribute these spiritual experiences to hallucinations brought upon by malnutrition and likely a lack of proper rest, but he was of the belief that unless you endure hardship and injury, you are not capable of experiencing such spiritual mysteries.

At the end of 1876, his father passed away at about 83 years of age and was buried near the mosque. From 1880-1884 the first four volumes of Mirza Ghulam Ahmad's work titled *Barahin-e-Ahmadiyya* reached publication, and the first covenant of his movement, known as the Ahmadiyya Movement, was formed on March 23rd of 1889. The adherents of the Ahmadiyya movement were considered heretics by both the Christians and the Muslims.

In the words of Hazrat Mir Muhammad Ismail[179] (d. 1912), Mirza Ghulam Ahmad had a fair complexion, well-

---

[178] "I imagined that these columns were an illustration of the mutual love between God and man. One light proceeded from the heart and ascended upwards and another light descended from above. When they two met they assumed the shape of a column." (*Mirza Ghulam Ahmad of Qadian*) p. 35.

[179] Otherwise known as Mirza Muhammad Ismail Qandahari and not to be confused with Sir Mirza Muhammad Ismail (d. 1959).

proportioned figure, and there were never any signs of grief on his face, but rather a smile that radiated with cheerfulness. His eyes always appeared to be half-closed which only added to the impression he gave of having keen insight and farsightedness.[180] Another account states that he was about 5ft. 8in tall, had a long black beard, and by the time he turned 50 years old, the beard had become entirely white.[181] He always spoke in a mild manner, except in one instance where he had raised his voice upon hearing of a legal case being brought against him, at which point he yelled:

"Will they persecute The Lion of God?"

The legal hearings proceeded. He was being framed for the attempted murder of a Christian missionary. Upon these allegations being proven false, Mirza Ghulam was offered a chance to sue for malicious prosecution, but he decided against it. He believed that they would face a higher power for their malicious intentions upon death.[182]

Ghulam was of the belief that Jesus/Isa had died of natural causes in India many years after his supposed crucifixion. His claim of Jesus having died a normal death is supported by his supposed discovery of the tomb of Jesus, located in the Indian state of Jammu and Kashmir.[183] Both the Christians and the Muslims strongly opposed this belief of Ghulam, because not only was he suggesting that the Christian belief

---

[180] The quote, as recorded in *The Promised Messiah* by Mirza Mubarak Ahmad read as follows:
"He was fair of complexion. His figure was well proportioned. No shock, grief, trial or tribulation could turn him pale. [...] There never was any sign of perplexity or grief on his face; the visitor always found a smile of cheerfulness playing on it. His eyes habitually remained half-closed. There was always an expression of keen insight, farsightedness and intelligence on his forehead." p. 11-12.

[181] "*Mirza Ghulam Ahmad of Qadian*" p. 4.

[182] Ibid p. 4-5.

[183] Ibid p. xii.

in his crucifixion was false but also that the Muslim belief that Isa had ascended to heaven while he was still alive, was also false. Ghulam refused to take credit for this finding, as he claimed it had been revealed to him by God. God had revealed that Jesus had only fainted when he was placed on the Cross, and when he was supposedly resurrected it was merely a matter of him regaining consciousness. Ghulam maintained that Jesus disappeared from Jerusalem but disagreed with his immediate ascension to heaven as a prophet. Instead, Ghulam believes he vanished from Galilee to India in search of Israel's lost tribes. Here Jesus lived a long life and met his death by natural causes in Kashmir where he is honored as the Prophet Yuz Asaph/Asaf, or 'Jesus the Gatherer.'[184] In the Ahmadiyya Movement the burial place of Jesus/Isa can be found in Roza Bal, a shrine located in Srinagar. According to those who overlook the shrine, the notion that it is the tomb of Jesus/Isa is absurd.

The devotion of Mirza Ghulam Ahmad is unquestionable, and his devotion is best shown in a statement that tells of all he would rather undergo if it meant he would not have to hear the ridicule that some use when speaking of the Holy Prophet Muhammad.

"God is my witness that if all my children, children's children, friends, colleagues, and helpers were slaughtered before my eyes, my limbs were torn apart, the pupils of my eyes were plucked out, all my designs were frustrated, and I was deprived of every pleasure and comfort, the agony imposed upon me by these on the Holy Prophet, peace and blessings of Allah be on him, would still far transcend the pain and suffering entailed by the miseries I have

---

[184] "*Mirza Ghulam Ahmad of Qadian*" p. 2-3.

enumerated."[185]

Throughout his lifetime, Ghulam gathered many followers, and the Ahmadiyya Movement has now been established in over one hundred countries.[186]

After spending twenty years of his life studying religion, Ghulam came to a conclusion. Of all the human virtues, truthfulness was the most important, and therefore integrity could be used to judge a religion, based on the emphasis the adherents of the religion placed on this virtue. In his estimation, no religion stresses truthfulness to the degree that Islam does. Some estimate that within his twenty years of study he had read the Qur'an 10,000 times. One thing he is known for having said was;

"Whenever I cannot understand something or am confronted with a difficulty, I forget about the difficulty and start praying to God – that solves the problem."[187]

Mirza Ghulam Ahmad was a prolific author, considering he had written upwards of eighty books in his lifetime, many of which were written in Urdu, some in Arabic, and others in Persian. A few of the books authored by Mirza Ghulam Ahmad, often authored under the name Hazrat Mirza Ghulam Ahmad, which merely denotes praise such as in saying 'your majesty' include *Kitab Al Bariyya* (An Account of Exoneration), *Barahin-e-Ahmadiyya* (Arguments in Support of the Book of Allah - the Qur'an, and the Prophethood of

---

[185] *"The Promised Messiah"* p. 20. In this instance, Mirza Ghulam Ahmad is speaking of the false claims and ridicule being used when speaking of the Holy Prophet Muhammad by Christian missionaries.

[186] "Among his followers are Nobel prizewinner, a former president of the General Assembly of the United Nations, government ministers, army and air force generals, doctors, scientists, millionaires, and millions of ordinary people from countries as diverse as Indonesia, the United States, Poland, China, and Spain. An immense missionary organization has established the Ahmadiyya Movement in 120 countries." *(Mirza Ghulam Ahmad of Qadian)* p. xi-xii.

[187] Ibid p. 44.

Muhammad) and *Aina-i-Kamalat-i-Islam* (A Mirror to the Wonders of Islam).

In *Barahin-i-Ahmadiyya* Mirza Ghulam Ahmad voices a challenge to anyone who can prove that their holy scripture is equal to the Holy Qur'an or anyone who can refute his arguments in favor of the Holy Qur'an. Anyone who felt up to the challenge, and won, would receive 10,000 rupees (155 USD), which would now amount to roughly 3,500 USD.[188] Nobody ever attempted his challenge.

In *Aina-i-Kamalat-i-Islam*[189] Ghulam impressed many with his explanation of verse 112 of Súrih 2 titled *Al-Baqarah* which states:
"Nay, whoever submits his whole self to Allah and is a doer of good, - He will get his reward with his Lord; On such shall be no fear, nor shall they grieve."[190]

Come December of 1891, Mirza Ghulam Ahmad published *Asmani Faisila(h)* (The Heavenly Decree), and in this decree, he describes the four qualifications of a true believer.[191] In September of 1893, he published *Shahadat-ul-Quran* (Testimony of the Holy Quran), and here he addresses questions regarding proof that he is indeed the Promised Messiah.

"The fact is that such claims cannot be proved comprehensively merely by means of reasoned arguments or documentary evidence, till the blessings of the claimant are established by heavenly assistance. This is the ancient law of God which has constantly applied to the prophets, peace be

---

[188] *"Barahin-e-Ahmadiyya"* p. 46.

[189] "Summary of Aainaa-e-Kamalaat-e-Islaam"

[190] *"The Holy Qur-an: English translation of the meanings and Commentary"* p. 45-46.

[191] "Summary of Asmani Faisila"

unto them."[192] – Mirza Ghulam Ahmad, *Shahadat-ul-Quran* p. 77.

Even Leo Tolstoy (d. 1910), often regarded as one of the greatest authors of all time, found pleasure in reading Ghulam's work.

Why would so many become such ardent followers of Mirza Ghulam Ahmad? Many Muslims were expecting the Mahdi to appear near the end of the 19th century, and not to mention that some Christian denominations believed that Jesus would reappear between late 19th and early 20th centuries.[193] Saviors are also expected to appear in times of war and sickness such as with the case of World War I and the Spanish flu epidemic. One must consider that the Ahmadiyya Movement has been one of the fastest growing Islamic sects in the world and that during this time of war, the son of Mirza Ghulam Ahmad, Mirza Basheer-ud-Din Mahmood Ahmad (d. 1965), was holding the position of second Caliph of the Ahmadiyya Movement. Mirza Basheer-ud-Din Mahmood Ahmad had succeeded Hakeem Noor-ud-Din (d. 1914) in 1914. At this time the Ahmadiyya movement was still young, having only been around for 25 years when Mirza Ghulam's son took his seat.

Mirza Ghulam died of natural causes in 1908 at the age of 73, and Hakeem Noor-ud-Din took his seat as first Caliph of the Ahmadiyya Movement. Nowadays, the Ahmadiyya Movement is led by Mirza Masroor Ahmad, the fifth successor of Mirza Ghulam Ahmad.

---

[192] *"Testimony of the Holy Quran"* p. 77.

[193] 19th century of the Christian Calendar or the 14th century of the Hegira. (*Mirza Ghulam Ahmad of Qadian*) p. 7.

# CONCLUSION

The idea of a Messiah, a Mahdi, has been around for ages and will continue to be around for generations to come because sacred scriptures tell us that we should anticipate their emergence. Scriptures warn us to beware of false prophets, who all too often lead us away from our previous ways of life. The words and actions of past prophets carry great significance for those who believe wholeheartedly in the message they represent. Because of this, I was able to write a book dedicated to a single messianic figure of whom we cannot even say with certainty has died or been born.

Imam Mahdi is an elusive individual, and we may never know who he was, is, or will be. His purpose is clear: to unite all religions under Islam. Whether we abide by or oppose the teachings of the Qur'an, we should be able to acknowledge that the term *Messiah* is not unique to Islam. Because of this, Mahdi is just another take on what we think will come at the end of time, assuming that time has an end.

The biographical accounts given in chapter IV only scratch the surface of Mahdi claimants of history. One may claim to be the promised Mahdi because they see that they can gain power through making such claims, whether that be militarily, spiritually, financially, or politically. One may also claim to be the promised Mahdi simply because they truly believe that they are indeed the promised Mahdi. This can be seen with the founding of Bábism, considering that it all began with a dream, a vision, and the significance that the Báb then placed behind it.

There are Mahdi claimants from all over the world, from different time periods, that enforced different laws, and used different tactics to gather the following that either continued after their death or died along with them. There are Mahdi claimants that may not have even lived long enough to make a mark on history. Muhammad Jaunpuri led through the act of performing miracles, the Báb led spiritually and through his writings, Muhammad Ahmad led militarily, and Mirza Ghulam Ahmad led through his books and knowledge of all primary religions.

Countless others deserved a place in this book, Bahá'u'lláh being one of them, but the accounts that have been covered throughout offer insight into what it means to be the promised Mahdi.

Has the Mahdi come and gone, is he here now, or has he yet to come? The world may never know.

# BIBLIOGRAPHY

Husaini, Ayatollah Sayyid Ali. "The Promised Savior: An Inquiry into the Imamate of Imam Mahdi (a.s) from the Viewpoint of Muslim Thinkers." *Internet Archive*. Web. Trans. Sayyid Abur Rauf Afzali. 1 Feb. 2015.

The Lahore Ahmadiyya Movement for the Propagation of Islam (Ahmadiyya Anjuman Isha'at-e-Islam, Lahore -- A.A.I.I.L.). "Summary of Aainaa-e-Kamalaat-e-Islaam." *Aaiil.org*. Web.

Hazrat Mirza Ghulam Ahmad. *Shahadat Al-Qur'an*. 1st ed., Ahmadiyya Anjuman Isha'at Islam Lahore Inc., 1989. *Aaiil.org*. Web.

The Lahore Ahmadiyya Movement for the Propagation of Islam (Ahmadiyya Anjuman Isha'at-e-Islam, Lahore -- A.A.I.I.L.). "Summary of Asmani Faisila." *Aaiil.org*. Web.

Hadrat Mirza Ghulam Ahmad of Qadian. *Fountain of Christianity (Chashma-e-Masihi)*. 3rd ed., Islam International Publications Limited 2007. *Alislam*. Web.

Hadrat Mirza Ghulam Ahmad of Qadian. *Barahin-e-Ahmadiyya: Arguments in Support of the Holy Quran & the Prophethood of the Holy Prophet Muhammad; Parts I & II.* 1st Trans. ed., Islam International Publications Limited, 2012. *Alislam.* Web.

Adamson, Iain. *Mirza Ghulam Ahmad of Qadian.* Elite International Publications Limited, 1989. *Internet Archive.* Web.

Jackson, H C. *Osman Digna.* Methuen & Co. LTD, 1926. *Internet Archive.* Web.

Bermann, Richard A. *The Mahdi of Allah: A Drama of the Sudan.* Cosimo Classics, 2010. Print.

Mirza Mubarak Ahmad. *The Promised Messiah.* Kent Publications, 1968. *Internet Archive.* Web.

Walbridge, John. *Naw-Rúz: The Bahá'í New Year.* George Ronald Pub Ltd, 1996. *Bahai-Library.* Web.

Walbridge, John. *Kitab-i-Panj Sha'n.* George Ronald Pub Ltd, 1996. *Bahai-Library.* Web.

Siyyid `Alí Muḥammad Shírází. *Dalá'il-i-Sab'ih (The Seven Proofs).* Translated by A. L. M. Nicholas and Peter Terry, vol. 3, 2008. *Bahai-Library.* Web.

Terry, Peter. *A Thematic Analysis and Summary of The Persian Bayán.* 1977, (Revised 2015). *Bahai-Library.* Web.

Imam Hafiz Abu Dawud Sulaiman bin Ash'ath, and Abu Khaliyl (USA). *English Translation of Sunan Abu Dawud.* Edited by Hafiz Abu Tahir Zubair 'Ali Za'i. Translated by Nasiruddin al-Khattab (Canada), First ed., vol. 4,

Darussalam, 2008. *Internet Archive*. Web.

Ahmad, Mirza Ghulam. "Darurat-ul-Imam: The Need For The Imam." *Internet Archive*. Web. Islam International Publications Ltd, 2007. Urdu version, 1989. Web.

Richardson, Joel. *Antichrist: Islam's Awaited Messiah*. Enumclaw: Pleasant Word, 2006. Print.

As-Sadr, Ayatullah Sayyid Muhammad Baqir, and Ayatullah Murtadha Mutahhari. "The Awaited Saviour." *Al-Islam*. Web. Islamic Seminary Publications.

Bowen, John Eliot. "The Conflict of East and West in Egypt." *Political Science Quarterly*, vol. 1, no. 2, 1886, pp. 295–335. *JSTOR*, JSTOR, www.jstor.org/stable/2138972.

Al-Samawi, Muhammad Al-Tijani. *Li- 'Akuna Ma 'Al Sadiqin: To Be with the Truthful*. Trans. Hasan M. Najafi. *Internet Archive*. Web. 2007.

Darmesteter, James. *The Mahdi: Past and Present*. Trans. Ada S. Ballin. New York: Harper & Brothers, 1885. Harper's Handy Ser. *Internet Archive*. Web.

Alam, Muzaffar, and Sanjay Subrahmanyam. *Writings of the Mughal World: Studies on Culture and Politics*. Columbia UP, 2011. Print.

Moin, A. Azfar. *The Millennial Sovereign: Sacred Kingship and Sainthood in Islam*. New York: Columbia UP, 2012. Print.

Campbell, James M. *Gazetteer of the Bombay Presidency*. Vol. IX Pt. II. Bombay/Mumbai: Government Central, 1899. *Internet Archive*. Web.

Sverdrup, George. "A Letter from the Mahdi Muhammad

Ahmad to General C. G. Gordon." *Journal of the American Oriental Society*, vol. 31, no. 4, 1911, pp. 368–388., www.jstor.org/stable/3087507.

Dr. Cormick, and E G. Browne. "Dr. Cormick's Accounts of His Personal Impressions of Mirza 'Ali Muhammad, The Bab," chapter in *Materials for the Study of the Babi Religion*. Cambridge: Cambridge UP, 1918. *Bahai-Library*. Web.

Nabíl-i-A`zam. *The Dawn-Breakers: Nabil's Narrative of the Early Days of the Baha'i Revelation*. Ed. Shoghi Effendi. Wilmette, IL: Baha'i Trust, 1970. Copyright 1932. *Bahai Studies*. Web.

Furnish, Timothy R. *Holiest Wars: Islamic Mahdis, Their Jihads, and Osama Bin Laden*. Westport, CT: Praeger, 2005. Print.

Melton, J. Gordon. *Faiths Across Time: 5,000 Years of Religious History*. Santa Barbara, CA: ABC-CLIO, 2014. Print.

Ahmad, Mirza Ghulam. "The Future of Islam." Sialkot, India. 2 Nov. 1904. *The Review of Religions*. Web.

Ali, Maulana Muhammad. *The Founder of the Ahmadiyya Movement: A Short Study*. Lahore: Ahmadiyya Anjuman Isha'at-I-Islam, 1976. *Forgotten Books*. Web.

Griswold, H. D. *The Messiah of Qadian: Being A Paper Read Before the Victoria Institute*. London: Harrison and Sons, 1905. *Forgotten Books*. Web.

Canney, Maurice A. *An Encyclopedia of Religions*. London: G. Routledge & Sons, 1921. Print. Classic Reprint Ser.

Masse, Henri. *Islam*. Trans. Halide Edib. New York: G.P. Putnam's Sons, 1938. *Internet Archive*. Web.

Hollister, John Norman. *The Shi'a of India*. Second ed. New

Delhi: Oriental Reprint Corporation, 1979. *Internet Archive*. Web.

Al-Tijani, Muhammad. *The Shia: The Real Followers of the Sunnah*. *Internet Archive*. Web.

Al-Bukhari, Muhammad. *Sahih Al-Bukhari (Hadith of Bukhari)*. Trans. Muhammad Muhsin Khan. Vol. 4. *Sacred-Texts*. Web.

*The Holy Qur-an: English Translation of the Meanings and Commentary*. King Fahd Holy Qur-an Printing Complex, Print.

Turner, Patricia, and Charles Russell Coulter. *Dictionary of Ancient Deities*. New York: Oxford UP, 2001. Print.

Sachedina, Abdulaziz Abdulhussein. *Islamic Messianism: The Idea of Mahdi in Twelver Shi'ism*. Albany: State U of New York Pr., 2012. Original 1981. Print.

# INDEX

`Abdu'l-Bahá, 44

'Abdu'l-Hamid Khan, 45

'Alí Khán-i-Máh-Kú'í, 47-48

'Alí-Qabl-i-Muḥammad, *See* Siyyid `Alí Muḥammad Shírází

'Uzayr/Ezra, 19

*A Mirror to the Wonders of Islam.* See *Aina-i-Kamalat-i-Islam*

Abraham, 11, 19, 36-37, 39

Abu Ishaq Shami, 17

Abu'l-Fazl ibn Mubarak, 26

Adam & Eve, 19

Afghanistan
    Farah, 27-28

Aḥmad ibn Muḥammad Qasṭallānī, 18

Ahmad Nizam Shah, 27

Ahmadiyya Movement, 75, 77-78, 80

*Aina-i-Kamalat-i-Islam*, 79

*Al-as-Sunna*, 15

Al-Baladhuri, 20

Al-Bayhaqi, 15

Al-Daraqutni, 16

Ali al-Hadi, 16

Ali al-Ridha, 16

Ali ibn al-Athir, 15

Ali ibn Husayn Zayn al-Abidin, 16

Allah, 8, 18-20, 36-37, 46, 57, 67, 77-78

Al-Masih ad-Dajjal, 11, 13, 19

*al-Mawahib al-Ladunniyyah*, 18

Al-Suyuti, 11, 26

*An Encyclopedia of Religions*, 19

Antichrist. *See* Al-Masih ad-Dajjal

Áqá Siyyid 'Alí, 30

Arab, 39, 62

Arabic, 78

*Asmani Faisila(h)*, 79

Australia
    Queensland, 21

Báb. *See* Siyyid `Alí Muḥammad Shírází

Báb's Bayan. *See* Persian Bayan

Bábís, 31-32, 41, 51-53

Bábism, 29-32, 82

Babu'l-Bab. *See* Mullá Husayn

Bada'uni, 26

Bahá'í, 53

Bahá'í Faith, 29

Bahá'u'lláh, 29, 41, 43, 48, 53, 83

Baqíyyatu'lláh. *See* Bahá'u'lláh

*Barahin-e-Ahmadiyya*, 75, 78

Baring, Sir. Evelyn., 61, 63

*Biographies of the Saints.* See *Tazkirat al-Awliyā*

*Book of Names. See Kitáb-i-Asmá'*

Browne, E. G., 47

Buddhism, 73

Caliph, 80

Canney, Maurice A., 19

China, 78

Christian, 11, 13, 70, 75, 76, 78, 80

Christianity, 11-12, 71, 73

Constantinople, 36, 56

Cross, 77

Crucifixion, 76

*Dala'il al-Khayrat*, 71

*Dalá'il-i-Sab'ih*, 48

*Dawn-Breakers*, 29-30, 32, 47, 51

Dawood, Abu, 14

Demon. *See* Jinn

Egypt, 60-61, 64-65, 68-69

Emperor Aurangzeb, 28

Fakhr al-Din al-Razi, 15, 20

Fatimah, 14, 16

Fazal Ahmad, 74

*Five Modes.* See *Kitab-i-Panj-Sha'n*

*Futuhul Ghaib*, 71

*Future of Islam*, 70

Garden of Eden, 19

Gate, 29-30, 33, 39, 43

God, 17, 23, 32-33, 35, 38, 40, 43, 48, 50, 53-54, 56, 58, 63, 66-67, 70, 73, 75-79

Grand Vazír of Náṣiri'd-Dín Sháh, 51

Green Island, 21-22

Hadith, 11, 71

Hajj, 26, 69

Hakeem Noor-ud-Din, 80

Hasan ibn Ali, 17

Háshimite, 35

Hazrat Mir Muhammad Ismail, 75

Heaven, 11, 17, 35, 70, 77, 79

*Heavenly Decree.* See *Asmani Faisila(h)*

Hegira, 80

Hind bint Abi Umayya. *See* Umm Salama

Hindu, 26, 70

Hinduism, 73

Hollister, John Norman, 15

Holy Bible
    Book of Revelation, 12
    Genesis, 32

Holy Prophet
    Muhammad, 8, 14, 16, 18, 71, 73, 77

Holy Qur'an
    Al- Fātiḥa, 71
    Al-A'rāf, 37
    Al-Baqarah, 19, 36, 37, 79
    Al-Kawthar/Al-Kauthar, 44

Aṣ-Ṣāffāt, 33
Maryam, 37
Va'l-'Asr/Al'Asr, 45
Yūsuf/Joseph, 32, 35
Hurmat Babi, 74
Husayn Hamadani, 47
Husayn ibn Ali, 16
Husayn Khan, 41-42, 45
Iblis, 13, 19, 50, 74
Ibn al-Khashshab, 20
Ibn Arabi, 20
Ibn Ḥajar al-'Asqalānī, 18
Ibn Hazm, 15
Ibn Majah, 16
Ibn Taymiyyah, 17, 20, 22
Ibrahim. *See* Abraham
Imam Ali, 16, 23
Imamate, 8, 14
Imám-Jum'ih, 45
India, 17, 26-27, 76-77
    Ahmedabad, 26
    Ahmednagar, 27
    Gujarat, 27
    Jammu and Kashmir,
        76
    Janupur, 26
    Kapurthala, 74
    Pattan, 26
    Qadian, 70
    Srinagar, 77
Indonesia, 78
Iran
    Chihríq, 49-50
    Isfahan, 23, 45-46
    Máh-Kú, 47-49
    Mazandaran, 31
    Milán, 47

Najaf, 35
Nayriz, 31
Shiraz, 30, 35, 38
Tabriz, 47, 50-51
Urúmíyyih, 49
Zanjan, 31
Zarand, 31
Iraq
    Baghdad, 36
    Hillah, 22-23
    Samarra, 22
Isa/Jesus, 11-12, 17, 19,
    22-23, 29, 36-38, 57,
    70, 76-77, 80
Islam, 6, 8, 11-12, 19, 21,
    30, 39, 41, 46, 56, 73,
    78, 80, 82
Israel, 19, 77
    Galilee, 77
    Jerusalem, 17, 77
Ja'far al-Sadiq, 16, 18
Jabál-i-Basít. *See* Iran
    (Máh-Kú)
Jesus the Gatherer. *See*
    Prophet Yuz
    Asaph/Asaf
Jew, 13, 36, 38
Jinn, 19
Ka'ab al-Ahbar, 12
Kaaba/Kab'ih, 39
Karím Khán-i-Qájár-i-
    Kirmání, 32
Khadra Island, 21
*Khasá'il-i-Sab'ih*, 40-41
Khidr, 19
*Khutbiy-i-Qahríyyih*, 51
*Kitab Al Bariyya*, 78

*Kitáb-i-Asmá'*, 53
*Kitab-i-Panj Sha'n*, 74
Kuthayyir, 23
Letters of the Living, 34, 36
Mahdavi, 26-27
Manúchihr Khán, 45
Mary/Maryam, 11
Masjid-i-Ílkhání, 33
*Masnavi*, 71
Minaret, 17
*Minhaj al-Sunna/Minhaj as-Sunnah an-Nabawiyyah*, 17, 22
*Mirát-i-Sikandari*, 27
Mírzá Abu'l Qásim, 35
Mirza Basheer-ud-Din Mahmood Ahmad, 80
Mirza Ghulam Ahmad, 70-71, 73-76, 78, 80, 83
Mirza Ghulam Murtaza, 70, 74
Mírzá Hádí, 34
Mírzá Ibráhím, 47
Mirza Masroor Ahmad, 80
Mirza Mubarak Ahmad, 71, 76
Mírzá Muḥammad Rawdih-Khán-i-Yazdí, 34
Mírzá Muḥammad-‘Alí, 47
Mírzá Muhít-i-Kirmání, 39
Mírzá Siyyid Ḥasan, 35

Moses, 11, 19, 36-37
Muhammad al-Baqir, 16
Muhammad al-Bukhari, 11, 20
Muhammad al-Jawad, 16
Muhammad al-Mahdi, 8, 9, 16-17, 22, 30
Muhammad al-Nafs al-Zakiyya, 23
Muhammad al-Tijani, 15, 19
Muhammad Baqir al-Sadr, 10
Muhammad bin Hasan al-Askari, 16, 18, 23, 30
Muḥammad Ḥasan, 34
Muhammad ibn al-Hanafiyyah, 23
Muhammad ibn Jarir al-Tabari, 18
Muhammad Jaunpuri, 26-27, 83
Muhammadan. *See* Muslim
Muḥammad-Báqir, 34
Muḥammad-i ‘Alíy-i-Qazvíní, 34
Mullá ‘Abdu'l-Vahháb-i-Qazvíní, 34
Mullá ‘Alí, 33-35
Mullá Aḥmad-i-Ibdal-i-Marághi'í, 34
Mullá 'Alíy-i-Bastámí, 34
Mullá Báqir-i-Tabrízí, 34
Mullá Ḥasan-i-Bajistání, 34

Mullá Husayn, 32-34, 38
Mullá Jalíl-i-Urúmí, 34
Mullá Mahmúd-i-Khú'í, 34
Mullá Muhammad, 50
Mullá Yusif-i-Ardibílí, 34
Murtadha Mutahhari, 10
Musa al-Kadhim, 16
Musalmán. *See* Muslim
Muslim, 6, 8-9, 11, 14-18, 20, 22-23, 26, 39, 56, 67, 70, 75-76, 80
Naw-Rúz, 53
Nicholas, A. L. M, 30-31, 35
Nimrod, 36
Nizámu'l-'Ulama', 50
Noah, 11, 19
Pemba Island, 21
Persia, 30-31, 35, 44
Persian (language), 78
*Persian Bayán*, 30, 48
Persian Gulf, 38
Pharaoh, 36-37
Poland, 78
*Promised Savior*, 15, 22
Prophet Yuz Asaph/Asaf, 77
Qá'im, 29, 33-34, 43
*Qayyúmu'l-Asmá*, 33
Quddús, 34, 38, 40, 41
Red Sea, 19, 21
*Revelations of the Unseen* See *Futuhul Ghaib*
Roza Bal, 77
Sa'ad al-Din Taftazani, 12, 17, 20

Sa'íd-i-Hindí, 34
Sabarmati River, 27
*Sahifiyi-i-Baynu'l-Haramayn*, 39
*Sahíh al-Bukhárí*, 11, 71
Sám Khán, 51
Sárá & Ahmad (wife & son of the Báb), 35
Satan. *See* Iblis
Saudi Arabia, 21
 Mecca, 17, 24, 26, 35, 38-39, 56, 69
 Medina, 23, 35, 38-39
 Mina, 39
 Mount Radwa, 23
Sayad Khondmir, 27
Sayad Muhammad, 27
Sayyid al-Himyarí, 23
*Sha'a*, 14
*Shahadat-ul-Quran*, 79
Shams-ud-Din Muzaffar Shah II, 27
Shaykh Ahmad, 31
Shaykh Tabarsí, 51
Shaykhís, 32
Shaykhism, 31
Shi'as/Shi'ites, 14
Shia, 8, 14, 17, 22-23
Sibt ibn al-Jawzi, 20
Sikhism, 73
Sir Mirza Muhammad Ismail, 75
Siyyid `Alí Muhammad Shírází, 29-53, 82-83
Siyyid Husayn-i-Yazdí, 34
Siyyid Kázim, 31-33

Siyyid Yaḥyáy-i-Darábí,
    44
Siyyids, 41
Siyyidu'sh-Shuhada', 49
Spain, 78
Spanish flu epidemic, 80
*Spiritual Couplets*. See
    *Masnavi*
Sufi, 23
Sufism, 23
Sultan Ahmad, 74
Sultan Mahmud Begada
    of Gujarat, 27
Sunna/Sunnah, 15
Sunni, 8, 14-15, 19
Sunnite, 14
Súrih of Mulk, 33
Súrih of Qarabat, 35
Syria
    Damascus, 17

Tablet of God, 38
Táhirih, 34
Tanzania, 21
*Tárikh-i-Jadíd*, 47
*Tazkirat al-Awliyá*, 71
*Testimony of the Holy Quran*.
    See *Shahadat-ul-Quran*
*To Be with the Truthful*, 19
Tolstoy, Leo, 80
Torah, 74
Umm Salama, 14
United States, 78
Urdu, 70, 78
Vedas, 71
Wali, 26
World War I, 80
World War II, 22
Yaḥyá Khán-i-Kurd, 49,
    50

# ABOUT THE AUTHOR

Alexander Ekwall picked up an interest in literature from a very early age and began carrying around a dictionary just about everywhere he went, to the point that it's now only held together thanks to the help of rubber bands. He decided to put pen to paper in high school as a means of self-expression and following his high school graduation picked up an interest in history and has not looked back since. February of 2016 marks the first edition of his newsletter titled *Omnia: A Little Bit of Everything* and *Mahdi: The Guided One; History & Controversy* is only the beginning of his writing career. Alexander Ekwall can be reached at this address:
alexwekwall@gmail.com
Website:
https://alexwekwall.wixsite.com/omniabyalexekwall